PRAISE FOR

Portrait of a Presidency: Patterns in My Life as President of The College of New Jersey

"Emily Dickinson once said, 'Hope is the thing with feathers that perches in the soul.' It should not be surprising that each chapter of Gitenstein's book begins with an inspiring quote from Dickinson. Gitenstein's journey as a stunningly successful pioneer in higher education—the first woman and first Jewish president of The College of New Jersey—should give us all great hope. At a time when educators are asking the question, 'Who wants to be a college president?' Gitenstein reflects on her long tenure as a leader and gives readers an inside look at her path to that role and her many challenges. What is incredibly refreshing about this memoir is her raw honesty about her mistakes, lessons learned, and her lust for learning. This inspiring book allows us to get to know a university president who is a decent human being, a highly regarded academic who loves ideas, and someone who has had a significant impact not just on her campus but on American higher education."

—**Freeman A. Hrabowski III**, ACE Centennial fellow, co-founder Meyerhoff Scholars Program; chair, President's Advisory Commission on Educational Excellence for African Americas (2012); 2023 NAS Public Welfare Medal, National Academy of Sciences; UMBC president emeritus; co-author, *The Resilient University* and *The Empowered University*

"A popular narrative today bemoans the college presidency as nearly impossible, a great burden that crushes even the most talented leaders. But R. Barbara Gitenstein's master work on the presidency tells a much different story, proclaiming the joy of collegiate leadership while illustrating the incomparable value of a great president in fostering institutional growth and change. From knowing how to pick a provost as a partner in academic transformation to comforting families and the campus in the aftermath of a tragic student death, to leading a traumatized community after 9/11, to negotiating budget cuts with the governor and state legislature, Gitenstein proved herself to be a strong, versatile leader for The College of New Jersey across the nineteen years of her stewardship.

"Long before they became hot-button issues throughout higher education, President Gitenstein dealt effectively with issues of freedom of speech, controversial speakers, and the complex web of diversity, equity, and inclusion. True to her belief that 'administration is simply another way of teaching,' Gitenstein's vivid memoir is an invaluable manual for new presidents eager to learn the nuances of a very challenging job. Experienced presidents will read the many case studies with frequent nods of recognition and cheers of support for Gitenstein's wise decisions and insightful analysis of challenges.

"In her final chapter Gitenstein summarizes the lessons of leadership she emulated across the years, including good communication, principled stances, smart talent acquisition, and generosity in praising others. To this excellent list I would simply add a large measure of gratitude for the privilege of the presidency."

—**Patricia McGuire**, president, Trinity Washington University since 1989; President's Distinguished Service Award, American Association of Catholic Colleges and Universities (2018); Carnegie Award for Academic Leadership, Carnegie Corporation (2015); frequently published in *The Wall Street Journal, The Chronicle of Higher Education, Inside Higher Education* and *The Washington Post*

"In her compelling memoir, *Portrait of a Presidency*, Dr. Gitenstein offers keen insights into the challenges of leading a large public institution. Through gripping renditions of her formative experiences leading The College of New Jersey for nineteen years, she imparts valuable lessons in leadership conveyed through honest self-evaluation. Those interested in becoming better leaders of character at work or in their homes and communities have much to learn from Dr. Gitenstein. Don't miss this opportunity to discover secrets to success behind key skills such as setting core values, mentoring, decision-making, solving complex problems, and much more."

—**Sandra L. Stosz**, vice admiral, US Coast Guard (retired), former superintendent of the US Coast Guard Academy, author of *Breaking Ice & Breaking Glass: Leading in Uncharted Waters*

"*Portrait of a Presidency* is a compelling account of a brave and intelligent woman's rise to the presidency of one of the nation's most remarkable colleges. But Gitenstein's memoir is far more than the narrative of a leader. It is a portrait of an era in American higher education, particularly public higher education, when one-time regional colleges could aspire to a level of excellence equal to that of elite private institutions. Under Gitenstein's leadership, The College of New Jersey achieved national prominence while still championing the 'ordinary extraordinary' students of New Jersey. Anyone committed to the premise that American democracy can be preserved through superior public higher education will find *Portrait of a Presidency* a source of insight and inspiration today and for the foreseeable future. It's also a great read!"

—**Terrence MacTaggart**, former chancellor, University of Maine system, Minnesota State University system, the University of Wisconsin-Superior

"With graceful language in nine chapters introduced by quotes from Emily Dickinson, Dr. Barbara 'Bobby' Gitenstein recalls and characterizes her life's journey. From childhood dreams of being an opera diva to student to professor to academic administrator to presidential candidate to university president, we follow along. She describes campus and family challenges with honesty, humor, and humility while not holding back in reflecting on her actions and commenting on those of others. She helps us see the challenges of balancing career, marriage, and motherhood.

"The title, *Portrait of a Presidency*, conveys the many-faceted dimensions of her story. It is the rendering of an academic life with vivid self-reflection; a portrayal of the challenges faced by a leader; and a series of vignettes that help the reader understand and appreciate the values guiding decisions made by the author. She generously acknowledges the roles and contributions of her senior team, members of the board of trustees, faculty and staff colleagues, and family in helping her navigate turbulent circumstances in what can be a lonely post.

"Dr. Gitenstein's nearly two decades as campus president included multiple crises, including 9/11, which affected so many lives in New Jersey; student deaths; controversies over the decision to rename a building because of its namesake's racist heritage; town–gown conflicts over the national aspirations of the college and its local origins; and political interference. It also included many milestones in student achievement and rising institutional prestige.

"This memoir is not only helpful in getting to know the author, but also it serves as a guide for future leaders in managing the challenges and joys of successful campus leadership.

"Dr. Gitenstein and I overlapped for one year in New Jersey, so I knew the institution she inherited and the environment in which she would be a leader. Her *Portrait* is a valuable addition to the literature on higher education in America."

—**Dr. Robert A. Scott**, president emeritus and university professor emeritus, Adelphi University, and president emeritus and professor emeritus, Ramapo College of New Jersey; co-author with Dr. Drew Bogner of *Letters to Students: What it Means to be a College Graduate*

"A primer on presidential leadership by one of the consummate practitioners of the art. *Portrait of a Presidency* offers an insightful, candid account of Bobby Gitenstein's long presidency at The College of New Jersey, an account grounded in wisdom, hard-won experience, and humor. A great read for a leader in any field."

—**Nancy Weiss Malkiel**, professor of history emeritus, Princeton University; dean of the college, 1987–2011; author of *Changing the Game: William G. Bowen and the Challenges of American Higher Education*

"Dr. Gitenstein's *Portrait of a Presidency* hit home like a ton of bricks. Ironically, we both retired from a leadership position on the very same day: July 1, 2018. We both spent decades, traveled hundreds of miles, and sat through countless, often painful search committee interviews ascending the academic ladder to the zenith. But it's what she accomplished during her nineteen-year tenure as president of The College of New Jersey that is truly remarkable.

"The book is an enlightening road map through the halls of academia. It serves as an insightful treatise for leaders in all fields of endeavor. A must-read!"

—**Stewart K. Lazow**, MD, DDS, FACS (retired), author of *A Surgeon's Memoir: 40 Years at the County*

"A nineteen-year tenure as president of a competitive college is an extraordinary achievement in modern American higher education. This autobiography describes and explains how and why.

"Barbara Gitenstein never stopped being a teacher and a gifted writer. Her narrative exemplifies the art of clarity in description and explanation—not only how problems/challenges were solved, but how rapidly they developed, often morphed into something very different, and quickly reached the level of complexity and impact that demanded the president's attention. The book provides a model of collaborative problem-solving and community building.

"Another rarity among leadership books is the importance Gitenstein devotes to her family life along with her professional responsibilities. There is a reality to this *Portrait of a Presidency* that is compelling."

—**Richard Jarvis**, chancellor emeritus, Nevada System of Higher Education; former provost and professor of geography, University of Texas at El Paso (retired)

"R. Barbara Gitenstein's *Portrait of a Presidency* is a thoughtful and unflinching memoir that peels back the layers of leadership in higher education. Through personal stories and professional reflections, Gitenstein captures the nuanced responsibilities, triumphs, and challenges she faced during her tenure as president of The College of New Jersey. The book is an honest portrayal of the profound personal and professional impact of such a role, offering readers a rare glimpse inside the so-called 'ivory tower.' Gitenstein's storytelling is rich with insights into strategic decision-making, campus crises, and the complex relationships that define a presidency. She balances the administrative and emotional aspects of leadership with remarkable candor, illustrating how the role intertwines with one's sense of self and family life. For anyone curious about the inner workings of academic leadership—or those aspiring to such roles—this memoir is both an eye-opening narrative and a source of inspiration."

—**Amy Hecht**, vice president for student affairs, Florida State University; former vice president for student affairs, The College of New Jersey; Pillar of the Profession, NASPA, 2024; co-editor, *The Next Act: Realigning Your Mindset, Purpose and Career*; co-author, *AVP: Leading from the Unique Role of Associate/Assistant Vice President for Student Affairs*

PRAISE FOR R. BARBARA GITENSTEIN'S
PREVIOUS WORK

Experience is the Angled Road: Memoir of an Academic

"Dr. Gitenstein has written a remarkably readable book about the people surrounding a young Jewish girl growing up in the Deep South. It is a warm but thoroughly honest account. This is an unflinchingly courageous story of love, exasperation, argument, and forgiveness. These are the events and people who shaped the woman who would become one of our nation's finest college presidents."

—**Thomas Kean**, Former Governor of the State of New Jersey (1982–1990), President, Drew University (1990–2005), Co-chair of the 9-11 Commission

"An intimate portrait of the journey to forge an extraordinary identity, R. Barbara Gitenstein's *Experience Is the Angled Road* depicts how a girl born into one of a very few Jewish families in a tiny Alabama town grew up to have a life filled with path-breaking accomplishments. Gitenstein became the first woman and first Jewish president of the College of New Jersey. The book moves like memory, with incidents accruing more meaning and detail with each repetition. Organized by chapters that focus on the most important people in Gitenstein's life, this memoir triggers the reader's own recollections, thus doubling its impact. It holds nothing back: painful rejections by lovers, hurtful estrangements from parents, betrayals by mentors, life-altering surgeries. But it also credits those who broke with the era's practices to encourage a woman and a Jew to resist traditional restraints and express all that was in her to realize."

—**Ellen G. Friedman**, Professor of English, Founding Director of Holocaust and Genocide Studies at the College of New Jersey, Faculty Advisor's Council for the Fortunoff Video Archive for Holocaust Testimonies at Yale University, author of *The Seven: A Family Holocaust Story* (a memoir) and many other books on literary criticism and Holocaust studies

"Vulnerable, candid, and inspiring, Gitenstein vividly portrays her struggle for emancipation from a cocoon of external expectations as a Jewish woman coming of age in Florala, Alabama, with dynamic prose and storytelling that will keep you turning the page."

—**George A. Pruitt**, President Emeritus and Board Distinguished Fellow, Thomas Edison State University

"We all are the sum of our angled experiences, but this memoir strikingly reveals the many sorts of experiences that make us what we are: family, culture, religion, time, place, friends, and the not so friendly. This is a moving, insightful, articulate, and intriguing exploration of all those forces and more. It will make readers more sensitive people."

—**G. B. Crump**, Professor Emeritus of English, University of Central Missouri, Fiction Editor Emeritus, Fiction Reader for *Pleiades: A Journal of New Writing*

"*Experience Is the Angled Road* is an engrossing, courageous, and touching memoir. This honest and poignant account describes how a bright and brave young girl with New York Jewish parents grew up in rural Alabama and, with extraordinary mettle, became an extraordinary leader of American higher education."

—**Patrick D. Cavanaugh**, Vice President for Business and Finance, Emeritus, University of the Pacific

"*Experience Is the Angled Road* is a poignant and insightful memoir. The author has captured, through letters and narrative, her own journey from being raised in a Jewish family in a small town in Alabama to becoming a college president at a time when neither was commonplace. With mishaps, wrong turns, and assumptions gone awry, *Experience* is simultaneously painful and inspiring. This book is full of *Ah-a!* moments, intriguing family members, and circumstances that are all too familiar, making it an introspective must-read."

—**Bird Jones**, Professor Emerita, Elon University, author *The Blue-Eyed Slave*

Portrait of a Presidency:
Patterns in My Life as President of The College of New Jersey

by R. Barbara Gitenstein

© Copyright 2025 R. Barbara Gitenstein

ISBN 979-8-88824-584-2

All rights reserved. No part of this publication may be reproduced, stored in a retrieval system, or transmitted in any form or by any means—electronic, mechanical, photocopy, recording, or any other—except for brief quotations in printed reviews, without the prior written permission of the author.

Published by

◤ köehlerbooks™

3705 Shore Drive
Virginia Beach, VA 23455
800-435-4811
www.koehlerbooks.com

portrait of a presidency

PATTERNS IN MY LIFE AS PRESIDENT OF
THE COLLEGE OF NEW JERSEY

R. Barbara Gitenstein

VIRGINIA BEACH
CAPE CHARLES

For Donald Hart, love of my life, and the reason I have succeeded at anything.

Table of Contents

Preface 1

Chapter 1: Dwelling in Possibility 3

Chapter 2: Life's Center 20

Chapter 3: Winter Afternoon Light 46

Chapter 4: Loss Again 58

Chapter 5: Props for the House 77

Chapter 6: The Pod of Revolution 94

Chapter 7: Selecting Your Own Society 107

Chapter 8: Both Ends of Remembrance 116

Chapter 9: Tell It Slant 133

Afterword 159

Acknowledgments 161

PREFACE

My first reflection on my path to leadership, *Experience is the Angled Road: Memoir of an Academic* (Koehler: 2022), focused on my great fortune in mentors, family, and friends who supported me; this book focuses on my great fortune to lead an institution that I dearly loved, to see it develop into one of the great successes in American public higher education, and to believe that part of the reason for that success was my leadership. As in my earlier years, I had extraordinary support from family, friends, and colleagues—both on and off the campus.

During my nineteen years at the helm of The College of New Jersey (TCNJ), I learned a lot about leadership and even more about myself. I had reconfirmed what I have believed since I was a teenager: higher education is the greatest promise for our country and for the world, but only if we nurture and preserve its values, values which are deeply seated in the liberal arts. We prepare students to become productive citizens, not just in the world of work, but also as members of society, individuals who can and should embrace the responsibilities of leading in an increasingly unsettled world.

This calling has never been for the self-serving leaders who are attracted to the position because of its influence, power, or compensation. And in these fraught times, it is not for the faint of heart. But when you are privileged to be a president at just the right place and just the right time, even in the most stressful times, it is a joy and a blessing.

This memoir is an accurate portrayal of my experience as leader at TCNJ, though there are some memories which are amalgams of multiple historical episodes and some fictional names which have been substituted for historical ones.

CHAPTER 1

Dwelling in Possibility

*I dwell in Possibility—
A fairer House than Prose—*

—Emily Dickinson

In 1990, after about fifteen years focused on the real business of higher education—teaching—I decided that perhaps my best contributions would be as an administrator. I approached the change with a lot of skepticism but with a strong feeling that administration was simply another way of teaching, and that if done well, it could be the platform for unimagined possibilities.

In some cases, there was no doubt that the students in my traditional classes were a lot smarter than some of the politicians I had to manage later in my career, but there were similarities in the work. Instead of teaching students how to write or how to explicate an Emily Dickinson poem, I was teaching faculty, staff, board members, political leaders, community leaders, and all those hovering parents about what constituted an effective educational experience.

I strove to help each of these stakeholders understand what I thought were their individual roles and responsibilities in effectuating the best experience for our students, not what satisfied the personal agenda of the stakeholder. I sought to share the opportunities afforded to us if we looked at things with a laser focus on what was best for the intellectual and social development of the students.

My first movement into administration happened while I was a faculty member at Central Missouri State University (CMSU). I held the job of the Executive Secretary of the Missouri Philological Association (MPA) in the early 1980s where I was responsible for receiving and organizing the submissions for the annual conference into sessions on similar topics. Since the submission process was an open one, the challenge was finding a place for some rather arcane topics and then organizing the submissions into panels of three to five twenty-minute presentations, trying to avoid conflicting panels on similar topics as much as possible for the day-and-a-half-long conference.

While CMSU hosted the first conference in 1976, in later years, other institutions in Missouri served as hosts. As executive secretary in those later years, I also worked closely with a liaison for the host institution to reserve space on the campus for the conference, including any plenary sessions, and overnight accommodations for the participants. Because the MPA did not have resources to pay for a publisher, we self-published the program, and I was in charge of working the light table to copy the text of the program and arrange for the printing of the photographed original at the CMSU printing shop. The name of the organization suggested both its breadth of interest and its vagueness of purpose, since "philology" allowed the program to encompass research on all types of literary criticism and a wide range of literatures and linguistics. The executive secretary position was not a position that had a lot of authority, but it did require organizational and interpersonal skills, all requisite for administration. I found that I liked the work.

My interest in administration grew when I met a group of remarkable women who transformed my expectations for my life in higher education. I spent several enlightening weeks at the 1983 HERS

Summer Institute for Women in Higher Education Administration at Bryn Mawr College. After returning to CMSU, I served for a year as assistant to the Dean of the College of Arts and Sciences, a largely undefined role, learning from Dr. Joseph Hatfield, Dean of the College.

One of my favorite memories was the time Joe asked me to represent the college at the Deans Council while he was out of town for a professional conference. I was excited to represent the college at the university level. I arrived at the private conference room attached to the office of the Dean of the School of Education about five minutes early. Sitting around a large highly polished conference table were three men who looked remarkably the same—middle-aged, paunchy, White. While they nodded in unison, none acknowledged my entry with a spoken greeting.

They returned to their conversation about the Kansas City Chiefs and the wonderful classical music of Ferrante and Teicher. Classical? Clearly, I had a different interpretation of musical genres. I kept trying to find a way into the conversation, a way to make my presence acknowledged. Finally, I offered, "I noticed that the agenda includes the discussion of a program to be added to the Department of English offerings."

"Oh, we won't be talking about that today. Since Joe is not going to be present, we'll just wait until he returns. We would want someone with authority to speak to the program, not a substitute representative."

Clearly, Dean Hatfield might have been foolish enough to think that a female assistant professor could represent him at this august council, but none of the other men around the table agreed with him.

For the next two hours, it was as if I were not even in the room. I was never able to distinguish well among the three individuals, and I was never given their names. The discussion never touched on the agenda, and the only controversial topic was whether it was going to storm the next day or not, depending on which television station had the best meteorologist. In some ways, the two-hour meeting was a complete waste of time; in other ways, I learned some important lessons about higher education and higher education administration, and particularly about higher education administration at CMSU.

I joined Joe for our regular bi-weekly meeting in his office two days after my adventure with the CMSU Deans Council. He had just returned from his history conference and was eager to hear of my experience. I turned to him and told him that I never wanted to go to a Deans Council meeting again. It had felt as if I were in the presence of a black hole, and I was afraid that the collective would just suck my brains out.

By the next spring, Virginia Radley, first female president of a State University of New York (SUNY) campus, one of the faculty members at the HERS Institute had suggested to the English Department at SUNY-Oswego that they interview me for a position. I was hired, and within a year, I had been elected chair of the department. I did not have clearly articulated plans for assuming an administrative role, but after the Bryn Mawr experience and getting some encouragement (from President Radley and from a couple of colleagues in the Oswego English Department), I decided to put my name up for consideration as chair of the department.

In some ways, being chair of an academic department is more difficult than being president of a college. Personal attachments and resentments complicate the chair's relationship with other faculty in a way that is largely foreign to a president. The Oswego department was a great case in point. It was large and fractious. One example of this atmosphere involved the tremendous animus against a particular faculty member. No one had trouble expressing their feelings, but no one could explain to me the source of the hatred. After I was elected chair, I spent one weekend in the office by myself, looking through file after file in the chair's office and never finding a clue.

It was just a foundational assumption: Everyone hated David Blissert. That is, everyone but me. Since I found him to be a dedicated teacher and highly productive scholar, once I became chair, I thought I would try to rectify the situation. I believed that if others actually worked with him, they would forget their previous animosity. I decided to ask David to serve on the search committee for a new position in American Literature.

Blissert was taken aback when I asked him to be a member of the committee but agreed to consider it, and two days later, he agreed to be part of the experiment. The first meeting of the committee was the next day. I went to that first meeting to charge the group, let them know the timeline, and give them a primer in search committee guidelines. When I entered the room, there were five people sitting around the conference table in the large conference room outside my office. Well, there were four people sitting around the conference table and David Blissert sitting on the periphery. The next morning, Professor Blissert walked into my office without an appointment and said that he was resigning from the committee. He walked out of my office without another word.

Because it was known that the president had recommended me as a candidate for the faculty position, there were those who had deep reservations about who I was, to whom I felt allegiance, and whether I could be trusted at all. I won the chair election, but by the slimmest of margins and in so doing created a group who immediately distrusted me even more. I began to learn some important lessons of administration—listen, listen, listen, stand your ground on principle, and when you can, seek allies.

In 1988, after President Radley had stepped down as president and Stephen Weber was named her successor, a number of administrative opportunities opened up. President Weber was looking for an assistant to the president and Provost Donald Mathieu was looking for an associate provost. While it was a heady opportunity to consider working in the president's office, I concluded that I needed to learn more about the academic enterprise if I wanted to continue to develop as a leader in higher education.

Donald Mathieu hired me in 1990 as Associate Provost. The fact that I was being considered for both these positions reinforced some suspicions of those in the English department who did not like my original ties with President Radley. As Associate Provost, I was fortunate to work for one of the best supervisors I ever had.

Those two years as Associate Provost at Oswego were some of the best and some of the worst years of my life as an administrator. Provost

Donald Mathieu, a great mentor, was as intelligent as Joe Hatfield, but he was more sophisticated and more knowledgeable about growing talent than Joe. He knew how to challenge those who reported to him, to give them assignments that helped grow their talent. Within a couple of months of my appointment, he reassigned the Office of Institutional Research and the Registrar's Office to report directly to me. Up until that point, I had had little professional experience with either function, but I learned.

After the formal office hours for administrative offices, I would spend time with Don and with another of his mentees, Paul Morman, Dean of Arts and Sciences. Don shared with us examples of difficult (sometimes humorous) personnel situations, and we shared with him our learning experiences in our new positions. The conversations could go on for hours. It was better than any graduate course in higher education administration.

Within a year, President Weber concluded that a provost who had worked well for a predecessor was not a good fit for his vision for Oswego. When he replaced Don Mathieu with another provost, I got the opportunity to work with a different kind of supervisor. While I learned from observing Don's successor, I found that just as Don Mathieu was not a good fit for Steve Weber, I was not a good fit for Don Mathieu's successor. I concluded that if I wanted to continue in administration, it was necessary for me to accept a job at the central office of SUNY in Albany. The academic year of 1991 to 1992 was a tough one, because I was working in Albany, NY and my family (my husband, Don Hart, and our two children, Pauline, age twelve, and Sam, age nine) remained in Oswego.

Since there was a threat of a winter storm for that weekend in January, I had taken the train from Albany to Syracuse, rather than drive home to be with the family over the weekend. On Monday morning, as I was preparing to return to Syracuse, my daughter Pauline stumbled down the stairs in the Oswego house to kiss me goodbye. In ten minutes, my son appeared, in his pajamas with a blanket. Don picked him up, took him down the stairs to the garage, and settled him in the back seat of the car. I slowly came down the stairs with the weekend bag that I took back and forth for the trips to and from Albany. I kissed the mezuzah and thought about how many hours before I could see the three of them again. It was wrenching for all of us, but I could not work with Don Mathieu's successor. That was clear.

It was snowing lightly, but I knew that whatever precipitation was occurring now, there could be a lake effect squall anytime. At least taking the train gave me another hour or so with Don and Sam and I did not have to cry for the first twenty minutes between Oswego and Fulton—as I did when I was driving and left the family together in Oswego. That only meant that the tears would start the minute Don kissed me goodbye at the Syracuse train station and Sam gave me that one last hug that had to last me for four days.

There was no way that I could have survived that year without Don, as he took on the full-time parenting of our children during the week. In fact, there was no way that I would have succeeded in my progressively more demanding administrative roles without him. Don is the most intellectually curious person I have ever met. He has an earned PhD in philosophy, but his undergraduate years were spent focusing on history and music. This breadth of understanding made him a natural leader in helping colleagues in the humanities learn how to integrate technology, particularly computing, into their teaching. Don's academic career began as a traditional professor of philosophy but later included positions working with computer-assisted instruction. He was always the voice of the faculty in my head during my administrative years, not in a limiting way, but in recognizing that what happens in the classroom is really all that matters. Don also knew what was at the heart of my sense of self and always advised me to choose the principled—not the expedient—way. He also always supported me in raising our family.

During my time as Associate Provost at Oswego and Assistant Provost at the SUNY system office, I learned from the challenges of working with the best (not only Don Mathieu, but my supervisor at SUNY central, Richard Jarvis) and with those whose leadership did not resonate with mine, what to do and what not to do, and I learned a great deal about the complexities of system administration. All of these experiences enhanced my resume so that by 1992, I was named Provost at Drake University.

The journey to the provost appointment was a hard-fought one. While I did not have a specific job in mind, I had become convinced that my next position should be in academic administration. I focused on opportunities in line (supervisory) academic administration. I spent almost two years interviewing for deanships and provostships at places all over the country, one year while working with Don Mathieu's successor, one year while working in Albany. The travel was exhausting.

The typical search at the time began with my identifying what I thought was a promising opportunity, then reaching out to a colleague and requesting that the colleague nominate me for the position. I would write an extensive response and application speaking to the specific qualifications described in the position description. If I made that first cut, I would participate in an "airport interview" (usually fewer than two hours in some nondescript hotel near a travel hub, with a search committee made up of representatives of all important stakeholder groups). If I made the second cut, I would travel to the campus for an on-site interview of two to three days. I frankly do not remember how many applications I sent out, how many airport interviews or even how many on site interviews I survived during that period, but I have vivid memories of some.

One day, I woke up in some motel bed and could not remember where I was. I could not remember the position for which I was interviewing. I reached over to the telephone by the bed and looked at the number, and read the area code: 404. Right, it must be Georgia State!

These interviews were more than trial by fire, they were amazing learning experiences that helped prepare me for the successful appointment at Drake, and eventually the presidency at The College of New Jersey.

There was one interview that I thought had gone very well. I really thought I had made some good points about my qualifications for the position. Two days after I returned home, Allan Ostar, the search consultant, called to let me know that I had not been included in the finalist list for the on-campus interview at the University of Vermont. I was disappointed, when Allan said, "You know, Bobby, you are a strong candidate, but the committee members felt you were not listening to them. They felt that you were not answering the questions they posed but rather providing the answers you wanted to give."

The one hour and forty-five minutes started coming back to me. The faculty member asked about leadership style, and I remembered talking about the importance of higher education in creating a knowledgeable electorate, the importance of a flagship institution in supporting state goals for education and social mobility, the power of research in the economic health of the state. Not one comment on leadership. I had not listened; I had not answered the question.

After this two-year journey, I was successful in the provost search at Drake University, where I would serve for seven years. During my years at Drake, I learned a number of truly important lessons. I learned the importance of principled leadership, describing myself in my first address to the university community as both an idealist and an intellectual. I tried to describe how I would approach problems that would come to my office; I also wanted to make clear to the community, particularly the faculty, that my perspective was informed by my disciplinary background. I consciously included quotations from important texts I had taught in the classroom. I quoted Henry Adams' tongue-in-cheek assertion that his experience in England in 1864 had prepared him "to act a fairly useful part in life as an Englishman, an ecclesiastic, and a contemporary of Chaucer." I quoted from Cynthia Ozick's *Cannibal Galaxy* (1983).

By citing the Adams quotation, I suggested to the community that the academy in general and Drake in particular needed to reconsider some of our basic premises. Just as Adams was an American, a man not at all committed to the life of the clergy and some 500 years younger than Chaucer, so did Drake and the academy need to look at its curriculum with eyes toward the twenty-first century, rather than the nineteenth century. We as academics and as academic leaders needed to push disciplinary boundaries and embrace collaboration, allowing those actions to enrich the learning environment. By citing Cynthia Ozick's *Cannibal Galaxy*, I hoped to suggest that simplistic formulae had to be rejected. A successful academic environment in 1992 had to be both eclectic and flexible. The citation also underlined my scholarly home, Jewish-American Literature. Simply, the citation of these texts suggested to the community that I was, at my core, an academic.

Themes from that first speech were woven through my tenure. By the time I left Drake, interdisciplinary study permeated most humanities programs and led to a revitalization and revamping of the general education program that all students took. Not only was I instrumental in redefining the academic direction and curriculum of Drake, but I also helped guide the institution through some serious financial downsizing. Some of my suggestions for administrative reorganization were implemented (the restructuring of the cabinet position of provost to include student affairs, human resources, and computing, as well as the traditional academic units); some were not (the restructuring of the colleges to create a single School of Professional Studies—incorporating Business and Public Administration, Education, and Journalism).

But most importantly, I learned to navigate two of the most difficult personnel matters that confront a university—the intercession with a faculty member who was suffering from end-stage alcoholism, and the negotiation of a resignation by a tenured faculty member. How a senior academic administrator manages negative personnel decisions reveals the leader's underlying values and principles. Even the most impaired should be treated with dignity and respect; even the most distinguished must be held to standards of integrity and honesty.

None of these accomplishments could have occurred without Don by my side throughout, not just giving me the advice that he had always given, but also taking over so many of the family responsibilities—cooking most family dinners (we almost always had dinner together), driving Pauline to and from Scattergood Friends School in West Branch, Iowa, where she boarded for high school, and driving Sam to and from violin lessons and bar mitzvah preparation classes. Don was perfect. Well, almost.

One night at around 6 p.m., I was sitting at home, exhausted after another day of trying to create strategies to meet the budget gap that was growing in the Drake budget. The discrepancy between the budgeted enrollment and how many students actually enrolled was devastating. I was struggling to get the faculty to understand that it simply did not make sense to continue to pay them full stipends for summer classes that had fewer than five students.

I needed a drink! The phone rang and I called to Don to see if he could answer it. I could not face one more person today.

"Oh, my God! Thanks, Sally," I heard Don say. And then an abrupt dropping of the phone.

Apparently, Sally Frank, a colleague from Drake, had found Sam outside the temple waiting to be picked up after his session with the rabbi in preparation for his bar mitzvah. Don had forgotten to pick him up.

President Michael Ferrari (Mick), one of my most important mentors, recognized my growing responsibility and success as an administrator at Drake by adding Executive Vice President to my title as Provost. As exciting as the opportunities Mick offered me at Drake were, I had come to realize in 1996 that I was ready to assume the chief executive role, to become a president of a college or university, to accept the challenge of being responsible for the entire enterprise. No one really understands the complexity of that responsibility until she assumes it, but my years as provost had exposed me to the core responsibilities of the university (academic and student affairs); I was fortunate to learn much about infrastructure and finance from my great colleague, Pat Cavanaugh (Vice President of Administration and Finance at Drake) and about community relations and fundraising from Mick and my colleague Don Adams (as Vice President of Student Affairs and later Assistant to the President at Drake).

The two years of interviewing for a position as president had many similarities to the two years that led to the provost appointment at Drake, but the competition was greater in the presidential searches and there were many more disappointments, opportunities where I thought I could have been successful, but where the committee did not. There were, as well, some situations where my desire to be a president spurred me to put my name in a search that was clearly not a good fit.

The search for the position of President of the University of South Dakota was a case in point. My first interaction with the search committee for the position, the off-site preliminary interview, should have been some hint to me that University of South Dakota was not for me. It was so cold that ice formed on the inside of the windows of the motel room in Sioux Falls, giving a whole new meaning to Midwestern winters. The committee members were members of the South Dakota Board of Regents, and their interest was in the impact of the system, not the university per se. During my months in Albany, I had had enough experience at the mother of all systems, SUNY, to be wary of such focus. But when I got that offer to interview on the Vermillion campus, I only knew one answer, and that was "yes."

A couple of weeks later, I had just been dropped off at the motel where I was staying. I looked around the bare room and thought, "Why, exactly, am I here?" When I got Don on the phone, he convinced me to stay, counseling me that the interview would be a great learning experience.

In thirty minutes, I was to be picked up for the first interview, and it was one of the most challenging ones because it was with the faculty. I thought they would surely have questions about my not coming from a Division I, flagship institution, but I was thinking, "Yes, but this is University of South Dakota, not University of Michigan." Not a good attitude.

As I walked into the large classroom for the interview, I knew this was not going to be a friendly crowd. The chair of the committee provided a short introduction detailing my credentials and then the questions from the faculty began—questions about managing scientific research programs, my success with getting money from national funders, and the date of my last published monograph. The interview was not quite as bad as root canal, but close.

Unlike any on-campus interview before (or after, for that matter), all finalists were on campus at the same time. On that first night, I was left on my own for dinner (also a first and last in my experience of interviewing). I decided to go to the motel's restaurant for dinner. I walked into the foyer of the restaurant, and there, right in front of me, were Bob and Carolyn Kindrick. Bob had hired me thirteen years earlier at CMSU when he had been chairman of the English Department. When I saw them, I knew at least one of the other candidates for the job.

"Bob and Carolyn, who would have thunk it? Bet I can guess why you are here, and you can guess why I am. What the hell, how about we have dinner together?"

In about a week, Bob and I both found out who the third candidate was when the University announced the appointment of former state assemblyman and USD alumnus, Jim Abbott. Bob and I never had a chance. The search committee and the Board of Regents probably knew the outcome of the search before Bob and I showed up at the off-site interviews in Sioux Falls.

Don's support and guidance were never more essential than in the months right after President Michael Ferrari announced in the spring of 1998 that he was leaving Drake for the chancellorship of Texas Christian University. I had mixed feelings about Mick's departure. On the one hand, I was excited about opportunities for presidential positions in other places; on the other hand, I had committed a lot to Drake, and I felt that I could offer the university good transitional leadership for the year it would likely take to conduct a national search for a permanent president.

During the years I was at Drake, the university combined some of the best qualities of the private sector and the best qualities of the public sector of higher education, becoming successful in private fundraising while at the same time attracting a more diverse student body, from urban as well as rural areas of the Midwest. It offered a wide range of professional programs in business, journalism, pharmacy, education, and law combined with quality liberal and fine arts programs to help prepare students to enter the world of work as well as the responsibilities of citizenship.

As provost, I came to understand the opportunities and the challenges of these combinations. It stood to reason that I had thoughts and hopes that the board would turn to me as provost to serve in an interim capacity as president. I was willing to stop all other searches and agree to focus on serving as interim the next year, deferring the opportunity of a permanent presidency someplace else.

At first, it seemed mere coincidence that Tammy Wynette died of a blood clot on the very same day that I was told that the Board of Trustees wanted me to come speak to them about the administrative transition at Drake. As the weeks progressed, however, I came to believe that these events were more than mere coincidence. Tammy was speaking to me from the grave and showing me the way. No one could have been more surprised at such a guardian angel than I, since my musical preference vacillated between Verdi and Motown; country music was, well, too country, for me. But during the spring and summer of 1998, Tammy Wynette's voice became the *cantus firmus* for my life and helped me chart my way to freedom.

Before that time, I could not remember ever consciously choosing to listen to country music—ever. Despite this historical fact, here I was in the middle of the workweek two months after my meeting with the Drake board, at the local Best Buy, looking at Tammy Wynette CDs. Browsing was one thing, buying quite another. So, it was almost an out of body experience to realize that I was walking out of the store with my very own copy of *Tammy's Anniversary Hits*.

I had heard Tammy Wynette in passing; I had surely never listened to a whole album or CD of her music. I opened the door of my Buick

Park Avenue, turned on the ignition, and popped the CD in the player where it played for the next two weeks. Her voice became the transition tune from home to work and work to home.

Mick's announcement that effective in three months, he would resign as president of Drake to become Chancellor of Texas Christian University had surprised the Board of Trustees. The timing was not great—Drake was experiencing the kind of financial challenges of all midsized privates in the Midwest; six months earlier, the university had announced an ambitious five-year $190 million capital campaign. And now, the president was leaving. The board was not amused, and that unhappiness made them suspicious of anyone who was as close to Mick as I had been.

I understood my job—stay away from board politics, make some of the tough decisions, and stand by Mick's side, showing the world I supported him. In normal circumstances, the Executive Vice President and Provost (me) would have been the logical choice for interim. Not this time, not this place. Instead, the board turned to the current board chair, the former governor of the state of Iowa, a Drake alumnus, Bob Ray. It was not just an unconventional appointment; the board wanted to make sure that the community understood who was in charge and that was the board, not some academic, and surely not someone closely tied to Mick Ferrari.

I didn't know whether the impulse to buy the CD to hear "Stand by Your Man" was energized by sick humor, self-flagellation, or contrariness, but during the first three days after the public announcement of President Ray, I listened to the tune about fifty times. I had memorized the words and found that the campy pleasure of mimicking the twang of the southern accent took me out of the reality of my day, out of the reality of my disappointment and anger. It's not clear to me exactly who "my man" was at this time—Mick or Drake, but in either case, I knew I had to get beyond those words, beyond the absurdity of pretending that the words made sense, but I was having a hard time finding my way and my own words.

One week after my unsuccessful talk with the Board of Trustees, I didn't hit the return button on my car CD after "Stand by Your Man." It was a Thursday, and I was relishing the idea of time at home away from the chaos that was Drake. I let the CD play into the next tune. The beat was the same, the voice timbre was the same, but Tammy was not making the promise to stand by her man. Before the end of the day, I knew every single word in the lyrics of "Your Good Girl's Gonna Go Bad" and my internal editor had kicked in big time. I had a plan. I was going to throw myself into the search for a position in sunnier climes, just like Mick. I was over Drake!

Then, disaster. One day in July 1998, I put the Tammy CD in my disk player, and nothing. The car dealer assured me that since the car was still under warranty, they would replace the CD player; unfortunately, the CD itself was likely destroyed. I tried to persuade myself that Tammy had already done her job. I did not need to hear her words playing on the CD. I convinced myself that I was going to be able to make the rest of the journey with her sounds only in my head. But in August, I got a call from someone at Stew Hansen Buick. They had received my Tammy Wynette CD back and strangely enough, it played just fine. After driving to the Buick dealership and picking up the reborn CD, I popped it back in the player and sang along as Tammy celebrated her plan to go bad.

By the time I participated in the off-site interview for the TCNJ presidency, I had become a veteran of the gauntlet of the interview process for a senior administrator in higher education. I had learned to answer the questions that were asked, not the questions I wanted to answer. And I had learned how to read a committee pretty well. Tammy's words were muted, but the idea of escape was not.

In mid-August 1998, I walked into a cramped room in the Holiday Inn Newark International Airport North. I was greeted warmly by a voice I recognized from the phone, Walter Chambers, Chair of the Search Committee, formerly Assistant Vice President of Human Resources at Bell Atlantic. The committee consisted of the usual representatives, but there was something different about the questions. The faculty members seemed more informed about the challenges of higher education; the board members were not only courteous, but also deeply committed to the special status of TCNJ; the students were simply amazing. I barely noticed the time pass.

After the final formalities of the interview, I ducked into the women's restroom off the lobby to change into my travel clothes. The next shuttle to the airport was in fifteen minutes. I needed to find a semi-secluded place in the lobby. I did not want to run into the next potential candidate unintentionally, though there was little guarantee that I would know for sure that some guy in a business suit was interviewing for the presidency of TCNJ. At 1 p.m., I stepped into the porte cochere of the motel and the shuttle was there. Once I got through security at the airport, I found a payphone to call Don to tell him just how right the interview felt.

Beyond the feeling in the room of the interview, there were certain features of TCNJ that convinced me that The College was the right fit for me. It was the right size (about 7,500 total full-time equivalent, or FTE, students); it had the right mixture of programs (pre-professional programs, but with a strong emphasis on the liberal arts, quality fine arts programs, and a commitment to excellent undergraduate education, including an award winning residential program that attracted "traditional" aged students); it was termed a "Public Ivy," meaning the school focused on attracting competitive students from the region; the campus was gorgeous (though a little too pristine and forced in its dedication to its Georgian architecture).

In addition, the campus had challenges that I felt were in sync with my own values and aspirations. There were opportunities to upgrade the curriculum, challenging the talented students and bringing in even more talented faculty; there were challenges to repair a relationship with a troubled but manageable local urban area (Trenton), challenges to diversify the student, faculty, and staff body, and challenges to rebuild trust of the board and faculty. These possibilities were enormous.

CHAPTER 2

Life's Center

Each Life Converges to some Centre—
—Emily Dickinson

Since I had been through the process before, I was prepared for the rigor and the constant scrutiny from every person who crossed my path during the on-campus interview for the TCNJ presidency. In this stage, Don joined me for the two-and-a-half-day visit, and we both took it as a good sign that the visit coincided with Don's (and our daughter Pauline's) birthday, September 19.

On the evening of our arrival, our sense of good fortune was tested. It was about 10 p.m. on the evening we arrived on campus and were ushered into the Brewster Apartment. The flights from Des Moines to Chicago and from Chicago to Newark, New Jersey were uneventful. Finally, we were on campus, but our bags were not; they were somewhere between Des Moines, Iowa and Newark, New Jersey.

Even after they were found, they would have to be transported the fifty miles from the Newark Airport to the Ewing, New Jersey campus. I was trying to imagine how I was going to make it through two and a half days of meetings in the same clothes I had worn for the flights. I was worried about whether I was going to look presentable, much less presidential. I was trying not to think about how likely it was that our luggage would arrive a day after we left. I really wanted this job. Don was his usual calm and reassuring self.

I had been tossing and turning for about three hours. It was 2 a.m. when the doorbell rang. And like magic when we looked outside on the porch of Brewster Apartment, there they were, our well-traveled bags. Not much time left for a real sleep, but at least I had clean clothes.

During the interview days, some of the time Don joined me for meetings, some of the time, he had individually scheduled meetings and tours. Don had much to share after his solo walks and interactions without me. We both found one particular detail humorous. It was a question that probably made sense if the spouse was the wife, but it did not make much sense since Don was not. The questioner wanted to know if Don had a preference for China patterns to use when we were entertaining at the presidential house. Don knows a lot about a lot of things; china patterns are not one of those things. On one of his walks, he scoped out the trailer behind the library and found that it was the sociology department. Apparently, no other candidate or spouse had even noticed it in previous visits. This became emblematic of Don's attention to detail and engagement in the least obvious aspects of The College. The community loved him for that.

On the second day of the interview, Harold Eickhoff, my predecessor, took me on a tour of the presidential house. It was a rather traditional four-bedroom home in a bedroom community, five miles from the campus. One of the expectations made clear to all candidates by the community and by the board was that entertaining of students, faculty, staff, alumni, and donors was part of the job. Whatever the reality of the house, the president and his or her family had to be flexible with opening their home. The Eickhoffs had been great models of how this should be done. They had regularly provided dinners for members of the TCNJ community, requiring reorganization of their living room, dining room, and family room to accommodate up to forty people for dinner, served by the institution's partner in food services but out of their family kitchen. There could be as many as three such events in a week.

During the final interview dinner with the Board of Trustees, Mr. Chambers, chair of the search committee, turned to me and asked about my feelings about entertaining at 110 Murphy Drive. In my mind, this was a question that required no thought whatsoever. I mean, if I wanted the job, the only answer was the one I gave: "No problem at all."

Apparently, my wardrobe and Don's performance were net positives, because after receiving a recommendation from the Presidential Search Committee to the chair of the board and a special meeting of the board, I received a phone call from Chairman Robert Gladstone offering me the job. I seemed to be on the cusp of owning my center, finding a home for my ideals and my hopes.

One month later, I was publicly named the fifteenth president of The College of New Jersey. I joined the board chair in the press room after the announcement. Everyone was giving me trinkets and tokens of welcome—T-shirts, keychains, teddy bears. Chairman Gladstone gave me a sweatshirt and asked me to put it on. I looked at the tag for the XL sweatshirt and almost laughed out loud: "Escape Wear: Get Out While You Can!" I would hear Tammy Wynnette in my ear.

The congratulations from colleagues, trustees, and friends on my being appointed president were heartfelt and deeply appreciated. The letter from Mick's daughter, Beth Masterson, was particularly pointed. She acknowledged the difficulties I had encountered at Drake recently and wished me an "uneventful" move and "a community that welcomes you with open arms." She proceeded to say: "You are an inspiration to women and to me—My father speaks of you often and well and I know he is so pleased you 'kept it together' (my words) and moved on to a more promising situation and experience . . . Go get 'em (Now, those are my father's words!)."

Throughout the process of the search, I had been receiving supportive messages from former SUNY-Oswego president Virginia

Radley, with whom I had had a conflicted relationship. At the beginning of my tenure at Oswego, she had been a wonderful mentor and supporter. Over the years, when I resisted some of her more intrusive tactics as an administrator, she became more circumspect in her support. While she was too sick at the time of the TCNJ search to write a formal letter of recommendation for the position, she sent me a copy of the ad with a scribble in her distinctive hand that she thought this was a good fit for me and that she knew the search consultant well and would be glad to speak on my behalf. The search consultant, Ron Stead, after the appointment was announced, echoed her sense of fit. He wrote, "I believe that both you and The College are big winners, as this is a terrific match." In Radley's season's greetings that year, she wrote a congratulations with her usual edge: "Congratulations! You have *it* along with its enormous responsibility."

After the months of stress and anger over the situation at Drake, I could bask in the kind comments that were part genuine and part performative from Drake University's faculty, staff, and trustees, few of whom had been public supporters for my taking on the interim presidency. From those who really cared, there were lots and lots of flowers. I have a photo that makes our home on Countryside Place in West Des Moines look a bit like a funeral home—five bouquets of flowers will do that. From October to the end of December, there were official Drake Administrative send-offs and more importantly truly celebratory moments—visits from dear friends from CMSU days (Lucy Blackburn and Gail Crump), meals with true friends from Drake, a celebration for our son, Sam, with his cohort who went through bar mitzvah training together, and lovely small lunches with close staff members.

When I was named president of TCNJ, I was fifty years old, Don and I had been married twenty-eight years, and Pauline and Sam were teenagers. Don and I were ready for this big move. Because Pauline had experienced two major moves in our family life and because she was already away at Earlham College, the move did not affect her much. Sam, on the other hand, had a traumatic change to process.

Don also had to acclimate to my assuming the presidency of a public institution. Since I was the CEO, there was not an opportunity to create a reporting structure for him to work at TCNJ without a clear conflict of interest. Fortunately, a colleague of mine who was president of Thomas Edison State College (later University) identified a position at his institution which was situated in Trenton, only eight miles from the TCNJ campus. The fit was not ideal for Don, but it was a positive and important learning situation for Don for the eight years that he worked there.

I was very much aware that I was on the cusp of a wonderful opportunity but also aware that my sense of self—as someone of outsider status (woman, southerner, Jew) with conflicting responsibilities (as an administrator, academic, mother, and wife)—influenced how I approached this opportunity. All of these conflicting reactions had an impact on how I managed the successful move. (The impact of the presidency on my family is discussed further in Chapter 7).

Three of the most important individuals in my success as provost were Marie Redig, my exceptional assistant at Drake, Wanda Everage, Assistant to the Provost, and Sandy Smeltzer, budget director in the provost office. Their congratulatory comments moved me. Marie described herself in the days after hearing the news of my appointment by saying that all she did was "keep smiling." Wanda wrote:

"You have been so much more to me than a 'boss.' You have been a mentor, a dear friend, and a wonderful gift from God . . . I am a proud Black woman and you respected that; however, you made me an even more proud Black woman because you continued to challenge me to become more than 'just' an Assistant to the Provost; you challenged me to become a colleague."

I had learned early on in my career that you are known as a leader by how you treat everyone, not just by how you treat those with status. Sandy Smeltzer wrote that she applied for the job in the provost office because of the way I had treated her when I first interviewed for the post at Drake. At the time, she was an assistant in the Dean of the Law

School's office. Dean of the Law School, David Walker, was the chair of the search committee for the provost at Drake and used his conference room for the interviews, so all candidates interacted with Sandy. She pointed out that when I had interviewed for provost, I was the only candidate for that job who acknowledged her as a person.

I took pride in being seen as a model for women and many of the staff particularly remembered that as they wished me well. A young member of the admissions office, Amy Nichols, wrote "Wow, here is a woman [who] leads with finesse, grace, and yet is also strong enough to be the only 'skirt' in the room and won't back down . . . you taught me many things—about being a professional woman, a wife, a mother, and also a working mother—I quietly watched you from the sidelines."

Even some faculty noted the importance of my position as a woman in authority becoming a president. Sally Frank, a well-known faculty member in the law school and the one who called when Don had forgotten to pick up Sam at the temple, wrote not only of my personal characteristics, but of my strong identification as a female and a Jewish leader. I was gratified that others recognized how important I found mentorship—not just as a mentee, but also as a mentor.

The storied Vice President of Student Affairs at Drake, Don Adams, remembered my first introduction as provost candidate, how I flourished as Mick's mentee and how I in turn mentored a number of young professionals during my years as provost.

Friends from my past reached out, including my office buddy from Chapel Hill, Wayne Pond, who hinted at the rivalry between UNC-CH and Duke University that my having been at Duke as an undergraduate (which he maintained was actually the University of New Jersey in Durham) helped me get the job in Jersey. Two of my most important academic mentors (C. Hugh Holman and Cecil Sheps) were very much on my mind. Hugh had been dead for seventeen years, but his close colleague, the famous literary scholar Louis Rubin, wrote that Hugh would have been proud of my accomplishments and that both he and Hugh admired those who would commit time and energy to administrative work: "If the good people don't do it, only the dolts and martinets will. Be good." Ann Sheps, Cecil's wife, wrote on his behalf, sending greetings and best wishes.

My trip to New Jersey to assume the position of President of TCNJ in January was not easy. First, I was going alone, as Don was staying with Sam to finish up the first semester of his junior year at West Des Moines High School. Moving a junior in high school was not ideal, moving him mid-year even less so, but leaving our son in Iowa was simply not a choice. Second, my leaving was in the midst of a ferocious Midwest ice storm. Finally, my predecessor was following the letter of his contract, not giving up residency in the president's house until the day before my tenure was to begin.

The board had concluded that while I had expressed our willingness to entertain in the current arrangement of 110, the board did not think that the house was adequate for what they envisioned. In the months before I became president, they passed a resolution requiring a major renovation to the president's house. Instead of moving into the president's house at 110 Murphy Drive, Pennington, I moved into Brewster Apartment, the small apartment on campus where Don and I had stayed during the on-campus interview. When Don and Sam joined me a week later, the three of us lived in the one-bedroom apartment for two weeks until the renovations of 110 were far enough along for living. The major renovation and addition, however, required that the family live in a construction site for six months. The construction crew was lovely but greeting them over my morning coffee every day through the back window of the kitchen was a little too much togetherness.

The College hired two women to help with the redecoration of the house, one for the public section of the house and one for the private section. These women did not get along, but the interior designer for the public section was a college employee, and she had strong opinions of her own about how the president's house should look. She felt little need to consult with me; I was totally fine with that. The other designer had different ideas about our relationship.

I had been on the job for fourteen days and I felt as if I were drinking out of a fire hydrant of information. I had a 10 a.m. appointment with the designer for the private portion of the house. As she walked in the front door of the house, I knew that her expectations were not mine. She wanted to know what my vision of the house was. My what? I had a vision for The College; I did not have a vision for the house. I politely let her know that what I needed her to do was to provide me two to three options that she thought would work for each room in the private part of the house. Then I could choose.

During the first couple of weeks on the job, there were minor surprises, and there were surprises which required major adjustments, some coming from the fact that I was moving from the private sector of higher education to the public side. When I was at Drake, the power of off-campus oversight was vested almost solely in the Board of Trustees. I had learned about that early in my tenure there.

On a summer night in 1993, Don and I were guests of Maddie Levitt, a Drake trustee and the first woman to chair a capital campaign for a co-educational institution of higher education in the nation. Her apartment overlooking Fleur Drive was filled with stunning pop art and elegant, low-slung furniture. That night, she wore one of her outrageous animal pins, which at first glance you might have thought was costume jewelry until the light caught one of the gems in the animal's eyes and you knew that it was a diamond. The view from her condo windows was spectacular. Mick and Jan Ferrari joined a group of Drake trustees and their partners as well as a couple of other city leaders.

Right before we left to go to a dinner at Skips, a local restaurant, Maddie turned to the group and introduced me and then asked me to make some comments. After thanking her, I commented on my hopes for Drake and my appreciation for those gathered in what they contributed to higher education in Iowa, their understanding of serving as fiduciaries—most were members of the Board at Drake.

David Kruidenier was a Drake trustee and a trustee at the more prestigious, smaller sister institution, Grinnell, fifty-five miles east of

Des Moines. At the time, Grinnell had already established its remarkable endowment, the second highest endowment per enrolled student in the nation. David was an exceptionally perceptive and supportive governing partner. David said he loved being a trustee at Drake because the work was so expansive. The trustees were concerned about enrollment, the physical plant, and the success of the next capital campaign. At Grinnell, he said they worried only about one thing: growing the endowment.

Bob Burnett, president of Meredith Corporation for many years, also a member of the Grinnell board, laughed and responded to my characterization of a trustee's job: "Actually, at Grinnell, we don't call ourselves fiduciaries; we call ourselves 'owners.'"

Moving to the public sector of higher education as an administrator from the private sector, particularly the regional public sector (rather than the flagship campus), was quite a transition with regard to board relations and influence on campus matters by those off campus. Because TCNJ was not Rutgers, our board did not include the kind of power players that would have been comparable to the Burnetts and the Kruideniers.

On the other hand, the New Jersey legislators were much more involved in institutional matters than the Iowa legislators were on the Drake campus. Some embraced the position of The College as a low-cost alternative to the kind of education that students would expect from an Ivy League school. People like Senator Peter Inverso were strong advocates for a program that came to be the most successful New Jersey vehicle for keeping the most talented students in the state for higher education, the Outstanding Scholar Recruitment Program (OSRP).

TCNJ and Rutgers attracted the majority of the students supported by that program. But some legislators (and a good number of College alumni) took a different view. They yearned for a time when TCNJ was one of several local public regionals. Many of them had attended the College themselves when it was less competitive to be admitted. They also coveted the role of helping get the children of their constituents into The College. When admissions standards got in the way, that threw a monkey wrench in their re-election campaigns.

Responding to trustee and elected officials' requests for special consideration for student admission became particularly challenging as the admission to The College became more competitive. At the beginning of my tenure, when I received such a letter of recommendation, I would offer to discuss the candidate with the Office of Admissions and would allow the Director of Admissions to take the lead after that. Sometimes, these cases were students who were well within the admission expectations of The College; they were obviously admitted. Sometimes, they were on the cusp of admission or had special rationale for admission; these candidates the Director of Admissions and I would discuss, and with the recommendation of the Office of Admissions, the student would often be admitted. Sometimes, they were not promising candidates and were not offered admissions because it was unfair to admit the student when there were serious concerns about success, and the student could be taking a slot that could be offered to a more promising candidate.

These negative decisions were hard on the students and their families. I came to learn that the rejections were not received well by the recommender either. Periodically, legislators would continue to pursue the request, but most often the request was merely a "check-off," as TCNJ's government affairs professional told me. They just had to be able to show the constituent that they had done something for the possible voter. In 2010, the New Jersey State Ethics Commission revised its training module for members of boards of trustees at public institutions of higher education to define admission recommendations to the institution of higher education for which the member served as a trustee as a conflict of interest. I saw this as an opportunity to manage legislative requests as well.

The trustees were not happy that they were no longer able to recommend children of friends and colleagues for admission, but it also meant I could use the change in ethics training to explain why we could not take trustee recommendations into consideration in admissions. In addition, I concluded that if this should pertain to trustees, it should also pertain to legislators. Thereafter, when an assemblyman or a senator wrote such a recommendation, the legislator would receive a letter from me indicating that I would no longer be engaging in admissions decisions. I simply forwarded the inquiry to the admissions office. Over the years, I got fewer and fewer of these special requests.

During the first week of my tenure as president, I began setting up meetings with my direct reports. The facilities staff had done a wonderful job of redesigning the president's office. Now there were shelves and shelves for books. With my Judaica collection firmly ensconced in the most public shelf and the intimidating desk replaced with a sleek table for a computer on the opposite side of the room from where Harold sat, I felt that the room was almost mine.

One of the first meetings was with Pete Mills, the Vice President of Finance and Administration. His span of control was extraordinary—budget and finance (which included financial aid), facilities management (which included maintenance, construction, and real estate), student services, and human resources. His tenure ended up being one of the longest in TCNJ administrative history (1971 to 2004, all but one of those years as a member of the president's cabinet). I began by asking him about the distinction between the boards of the Trenton State College (TSC) Corporation and the TCNJ Foundation.

"Well, the Corporation is a separate entity from The College. It owns and manages the properties in Ewing and other land in the name of The College. Most of the rental properties were intended for faculty and staff living. The foundation is the locus for fundraising at The College."

I then asked him about how we were covering the cost of the salary increases for unionized employees negotiated by the governor's office. I remembered during my interview that someone emphasized that since the majority of our employees were unionized, this would be a huge hit to our budget. But I did not see in the budget documents where that negotiated amount had been added to our state appropriation. How could the governor negotiate but then not allocate? Pete answered that the increases had to be covered by budget reduction, tuition increase, or both.

I tried to process this new concept in "state appropriation think,"—

negotiating for a sizable increase in expenses without providing resources to cover that expense, leaving the individual institution to either raise tuition or cut programs. Seemed unfair. Well, welcome to public higher education, I learned. I went to the next topic on my budgetary agenda—financial aid and the size of the merit-based scholarship program.

"Bobby, you really do not need to understand all of that. Harold always let me manage all these details and you should as well."

"Well, Pete, I am not Harold."

I learned in the early months of my tenure as president just how important it was for me to be seen and heard, to speak to the community at large, to share what I had learned so far, and to set expectations. A month after taking office, I gave my first speech to the community. While most of the audience was faculty and staff, the speech was open to faculty, students, staff, and board members.

I had to articulate what part of the principles and parameters embraced by my predecessor would be foundational to my sense of the future of TCNJ and what I thought needed to be reconsidered. Rather than defining our quality by the high SAT scores of incoming students, I wanted the community to define our success in terms of graduation rates and job and graduate school placements; I urged us to focus more on academic program development rather than physical plant improvement. In the end, we needed to embrace thoughtful risk.

I also emphasized the importance of real communication between and among all stakeholder groups, particularly the faculty and the administration which had become seriously frayed in the last years of Harold Eickhoff's tenure: "Every community has its own history and language, but those symbols and sounds can change and where we think they should change, let us make those changes. Remember at this particular juncture, I do not yet share a history, or a symbol set with you."

I ended the speech with a quotation from an Emily Dickinson poem, a practice that became a tradition for my speeches to the community. I rewrote her vision of how aspiration grows just as a cocoon morphs into a butterfly, mirroring the promise I saw in TCNJ's future.

Beginning in the second semester of my tenure as president and continuing for almost three years, the campus was struck by several campus crises that tested me as a new president. A good number of the incidents were bias incidents (racial, antisemitic, and homophobic); some focused more directly on freedom of expression with regard to patriotic identification, hate speech, and off-color parody.

In September 1999, The College was informed of a parody website criticizing the administration, particularly me as president, using Nazi symbolism. This was frightening in itself, as it was the first time I as an administrator had been targeted with specifically antisemitic comments. More significantly, it coincided with my inauguration in October 1999, and there were concerns that the verbal threats would bleed out into some larger action to hurt the community and the celebration. As it turned out, the almost incoherent writings were the result of a single individual who was unhappy about a student disciplinary action, but the impact on the campus, particularly the Jewish community, was significant.

In February 2000, an invitation to join a Church of Satan organization was posted in Travers Hall, one of the freshman residence halls. In March 2000, the Black Student Union received threatening emails. In early fall 2000, swastikas and racial slurs were found on walls and stairwells in one of the freshman dormitories and rumors of black-clad young men roaming the campus began circulating. In October 2000, the Jewish Student Organization (JSO) received a threatening email filled with antisemitic tropes and threats. In spring of 2001, a student reported receiving homophobic messages.

The most problematic of these several episodes were the series of racial attacks and the threatening emails to the JSO, because they implied violence. As each of these episodes occurred, they seemed to be discrete and unrelated, but the impact was cumulative. A new president was being challenged, and I had to think through each incident and develop a plan that was both responsive to that particular threat as well as cognizant of its historical context. Where a culprit could be identified (with regard to the racist and antisemitic episodes), a full range of legal or counseling actions was taken, depending on the facts of the case and the severity and prevalence of the action. Where a posting was determined to be covered by the first amendment (the parody website), educational and community-building activities were implemented. There were, of course, those who found our reactions either too nuanced or too liberal, but each episode had its own set of facts. What they shared was an underlying prejudice against "the other."

In some ways, the most difficult of these episodes to manage was the accusation of homophobic bullying, since it was discovered that the accusation was a hoax; the student victim was the one who sent the messages. It was important that our response in this case was to share the facts that we could take appropriate disciplinary action (which had to remain confidential), and make clear the institutional position on bullying, whoever the perpetrator. It did not matter who sent the message; the TCNJ community, particularly the targeted community, felt threatened.

Early in the series of these episodes, a rally was planned by the Black Student Union and members of the administration. A crowd of close to a thousand filled the quad from the student center to the admissions building. The provost had announced that classes would be canceled from 2:00 to 3:20 p.m. for the community to gather together to speak out against the recent bias incidents. The student leadership requested that I join them on the dais. As I looked out over the faces, I felt incredibly uncomfortable, though I could not put my finger on why. I believe that the invitation to sit on the dais was an expression of confidence in me as the new president. Nevertheless, I felt a sense of disquiet.

Two days after the rally, I had a scheduled meeting with New Jersey's Secretary of State, DeForest Blake "Buster" Soaries. He was a well-known community leader and preacher at the First Baptist Church of Lincoln Gardens in Somerset, NJ. After welcoming me to the state, Reverend Soaries commented:

"Before we start talking about your vision for The College, I have to comment on the protest on your campus a couple of days ago. As

I think you know, I have sort of a history of political protests on a number of topics, including, of course, racial disparity. I thought your students were remarkably well behaved. I will tell you that in my day, I would likely not have been so well behaved."

I realized that neither would I have been. Suddenly, I understood my discomfort sitting on that dais. I had had a good bit of experience as a student protester; that day was my first as a president hearing student protest.

In November 2001, an American flag was removed from a residence hall window. Only two months after 9/11, the reaction was immediate and indignant—not just locally, but also nationally. The rationale for the removal of the flag was that it was a fire hazard. Two emails captured the feelings of those who objected to the administrative action. One read, "As a taxpayer and a New Jersey resident who pays $10,000 per year in property taxes, $6,500 of which goes to education, I demand you rethink this asinine ruling. I am sick and tired of anti-American attitudes on our country's college campuses." The second, more moderate one read, "As a 'child of the '60s,' I have watched the recent outpouring of patriotism with a sense of awe and wonder." The author could not, however, understand The College's decision to remove the flag.

In April 2002, the disappearance of a stack of student newspapers from the student union before the April Student Acceptance Day, the largest admissions event of the year, drew similar outrage, though not at the national level. The students, particularly the writers for the student newspaper, were outraged by the removal of the *Signal*. It turned out that the action was a well-meaning, but ill-conceived action by a staff member who found the April 1 parody publication, the *Singal*, particularly outrageous that year and worried that it might offend prospective parents and students.

In both cases, TCNJ's administrative response was overbearing, infantilizing both the students and the community. While I was not personally involved in either of these actions, I learned that no administrative action can be separated from the president. I had to be seen as being part of undoing both these administrative actions. With regard to the removal of the flag, the student was informed that he could (with safety restrictions) be allowed to rehang his flag. With regard to the removal of the student newspapers, we replaced the issues of the *Signal* (and the *Singal*), assuring that they were available on Student Acceptance Day.

These flare ups, however, paled in comparison to the fallout from the visit of Reverend Stephen White, a local Pentecostal preacher. One year and five days after 9/11, Reverend White, registered to speak on the TCNJ campus, using the typical procedures which informed officials in Student Affairs and the campus police. At the time, the campus community was not aware of his reputation for incendiary speech. Since I was not on campus that day as it was Yom Kippur, I was not privy to the volatility myself.

White set up shop on the planter in front of Brower Student Center in the middle of the day where he was sure to be seen and heard by the largest number of students and faculty as they changed classes and went to lunch. His visit elicited both the best and the worst in our community. His words were filled with the most offensive sexist, racist, homophobic, antisemitic, and anti-immigrant rhetoric. As he spewed his hate for an hour, student emotions grew. In some cases, students tried to engage him in discussion. In most cases, they angrily tried to shout him down. By the time that White left, some in the community had keyed his car. White had gotten what he sought—a great story that was plastered all over the local press the next day.

What shocked me most was not the angry outcry on campus, but the call for me to have denied White the right to speak on campus. It became clear that I needed to communicate with the campus about my decision making. I asked the *Signal* to publish a message to the campus, in which I began by delineating the several routes whereby controversial speakers come to campus, expressing concern about establishing a protocol to limit speech by administrative fiat:

Perhaps there is wide consensus on this individual, but what about Rush Limbaugh, Al Sharpton, Winnie Mandela, Jerry Falwell, Louis Farrakhan, Ariel Sharon, or Yasser Arafat? What guidelines should we use in these cases? I am also confident that The College would have substantial legal obstacles in developing such guidelines . . .

We must encourage all community members to speak for themselves, to be able to hear an unacceptable viewpoint and respond . . . Speaking out fervently and passionately, citing contrary opinions, trying to engage the speaker in debate—all constitute such acceptable response. So does silence and absence . . . Whereas such speech, silence, and absence constitute acceptable response, violence, and vandalism do not . . .

I ended by expressing my personal objection to the opinions of Reverend White, but those personal opinions did not mean that I as president should silence someone by denying him access to the campus simply because of his words.

These types of experiences, some of the most challenging in my tenure, continued during my time as president. In my last year as president, a group called the Bible Believers, espousing similar beliefs to those of Reverend White, informed the campus police that they would be speaking in the Alumni Grove between the library and Eickhoff Hall, the main student cafeteria. While there was a heated student and faculty response to this episode, the community did not devolve into violence or vandalism.

The next day, The College held its spring "Critical Conversation" led by administrators in Student Affairs and the Office of Diversity and Inclusion, providing a forum for understanding the institutional policy on outside speakers and the power of civil protest. A couple of days later, this same group held a Diversity Celebration, echoing the Michelle Obama quotation, "When they go low, we go high," allowing student leaders to speak of their celebration of individual identity and their rejection of the kind of hate and xenophobia that permeated the remarks of the Bible Believers. It was truly gratifying to see just how much the community had learned since Reverend White's visit in 2002 in how to respond to such offensive speech.

The most complex local crisis that I had to confront during my years as president was in the 2016 to 2017 academic year. In early December, Provost Jacqueline Taylor informed me that a group of students doing community research in a history class had uncovered the unsavory history of a former superintendent of schools in Trenton, who served from 1932 to 1955, for whom a building on the campus was named.

A group of students began posting unsigned flyers on campus describing Paul Loser (pronounced with a long "o") as a racist. Immediately, I sent out a message to the campus acknowledging the postings and sharing that I would be meeting with the students who had been doing research on the matter. I scheduled a meeting with the faculty advisor, the student researchers, and other academic and student affairs leadership to acknowledge the shared concerns and to promise action, though I pointed out we would likely wait until after exams and mid-winter break to engage in a thorough study process.

In the meantime, I began conducting my own research, discovering that this was not the first time a student researcher had uncovered Paul Loser's past, but it had never made it past the individual classroom. Working with the Vice President for College Advancement, we began strategizing for a plan of action. By January, we announced the establishment of the Advisory Commission on Social Justice, Race, and Educational Attainment, a sixteen-member group that included faculty, students, staff, and community members (including Walter Chambers, chair of the Search Committee that recommended my appointment as president and former Chair of the Board of Trustees). The commission was co-chaired by Vice President Donohue and a distinguished history professor, Dr. Chris Fisher.

The charge for the Commission was to look not only at the issue of Paul Loser's history but also to consider the relationship of The College to the city of Trenton. This is a tortured history. The New Jersey State

Normal School (the first name of the institution that eventually became TCNJ) opened its doors in 1855, located on Clinton Avenue in downtown Trenton. In 1928, land for a new site was purchased on the outskirts of the city, in Ewing Township, and by the early 1930s, the institution had moved to its new suburban site.

The physical move and a series of name changes came to be viewed by some residents of Trenton as attempts to distance the institution from the city because of its racial makeup and because of its social and economic challenges. Over the years, there have been six names for the institution, all but the first and the last with Trenton as part of the institution's name. Trenton State College, the name from 1958 to1995, helped cement the relationship between the institution and the city, despite the change in location to outside of the city.

The change of the name to The College of New Jersey in 1996 precipitated a lawsuit with Princeton University, which up until the late 1800s had been known as The College of New Jersey. The lawsuit with Princeton was settled before my time as president. The judgment required that while we could use the name, we could never juxtapose the name with the date of our establishment in 1855 (as Princeton was The College of New Jersey at that time). The 1996 name change also fueled a great deal of alumni and community anger.

There were strong feelings that the name signaled a move from a regional institution serving families in the local community to a competitive college that drew the most academically talented students from across the state and beyond. It was seen as part and parcel of an attempt to divorce the school from its past and its relationship to Trenton. The fact that the choice of the new name poked the neighboring Ivy League colleague only added to that conclusion.

When I arrived at TCNJ, three years after the name change, the heat of the argument still fueled many discussions with alumni and most of the political leadership of Trenton and central Jersey. Some of the arguments were cogent recognition of a failure of the institution to support the needs of the increasingly difficult social and financial strains on the city. Some of the arguments were not.

My first full academic year as president, I attended the New Jersey Education Association (NJEA) Convention in Atlantic City. As I entered the exhibition hall, I looked for TCNJ's booth. There we were in the middle aisle with a nice booth decorated with lots of posters and swag emblazoned with the logo and emblems of The College. I greeted the TCNJ representative who was manning the booth and asked how the crowds had been.

A middle-aged woman approached us.

"Just to let you know, I am a proud alumna of Trenton State College, and I will never ever give you a penny until you change the name back to TSC. Never."

I knew from experience that when someone started out the conversation with, "I will never give you a penny until [fill in the blank]," that person likely had never given a penny to the college. Nevertheless, it was my job to be polite and politic.

I introduced myself as the new president and tried to engage with her, acknowledging her feelings, but assuring her that we embraced our past, even as we embraced our future with a new name. I asked for her name and date of graduation. When I found out that she was a 1992 elementary education alumna, I invited her back to the campus to see what we were doing in leading edge educational practices and to meet with her former faculty members. She was not interested. Before she left, I told her that we were keeping a record of who visited the booth and would like to know her name at graduation.

When she gave a different last name from her current one, I replied. "Ah, so you changed your name, too!"

As I was conducting my own research on the Loser Hall situation, I reached out to colleagues who had experienced similar challenges. President Jack DeGioia navigated a masterful response at Georgetown University to its complex history of slave ownership; President Chris Eisgruber led Princeton University in its response to the problematic history of Woodrow Wilson's support of segregation throughout his political and public career, even during his years as president of the United States. Wilson's name was on a school, a major institute, and facilities across the Princeton campus. I learned from these colleagues the importance of being responsive to the specifics of the situation, but also thinking into the future—what would be or should be the long-term impact of such an initiative? The goal should be to change the organization for the long run, to go beyond the cosmetic.

I entered into the process with a strong feeling that changing the name of an asset should be approached with caution. Such a change would set a precedent for undoing historical actions and dishonoring agreements. I also had a close personal relationship with the Loser family. I had never known Dr. Paul Loser, but I did know his son, Tom, and his daughter in law, Carol, who had been exceptionally generous and kind to The College. However, by the time I had done my own research (even before the final recommendation from the commission), I was convinced that the question was not what it would mean to change the name, but what it would mean to keep the name.

In February, I hosted a private luncheon with Carol Loser (Tom had died three years earlier), during which I planned to explain to her my rationale for supporting the idea of changing the name of the hall. A student assistant met Carol at the guest parking lot near Loser Hall and walked her to my office where we could talk with complete privacy. When she arrived, I hugged her. After the usual pleasantries, I broached the subject that we both knew had to be discussed.

"You know, Bobby, I really had no sense of this aspect of my father-in-law. I knew him as an educational leader and as the father of Tom, who loved him very much. I just had no idea. I know that sounds unbelievable, but it's true."

I then let her know that I had been doing some of my own research and unfortunately had found my conclusions were the same as what she had been reading in the press. Dr. Loser's actions were—there's just no other word for it—racist. I was sorry to have had that confirmed for me. And even more sorry that I had to share that opinion with her, someone whom I so admired, someone who had been so supportive of TCNJ and women's leadership.

Carol looked down. "I understand, and I also understand that you will have to take the action of removing the Loser name from the building. I just hate it. I am glad that Tom is not around to know that this is happening, but you will not hear anything else from me about this situation and I will *not* speak to anyone in the press. I will make no public statements."

Paul Loser had been Superintendent of Schools in Trenton for over twenty years. His legacy in the community was deep and long. The African American community was shocked, not by the information included in the student research, but that this was news. Their lived lives proved more details than any TCNJ student could uncover. In fact, the TCNJ community should not have been shocked. There were two TCNJ students who had written of the situation in the Trenton school system in past years (Lauren Wells and Trevor McLaughlin); there was a 1959 Rutgers EdD thesis on the topic (Roland Howard Daniels). In the April 2013 issue of The TCNJ *Journal of Student Scholarship* (Volume XV), Trevor McLaughlin, under the supervision of Robert McGreevey, of TCNJ's History Department, published "A View from the Chalkboard: Trenton School Desegregation and the Struggle of Black Teachers in the Pre-Brown Era, 1944-1954," a thorough analysis of the segregation of the teaching ranks in Trenton, which included many of the same facts that energized the student protest in 2016. In addition, the faculty sponsor of that research was the same faculty sponsor of the research in 2016.

The facts included the following: In 1881, New Jersey passed a law that prohibited the placement of students in schools based on the color of their skin, one of the first such laws in the nation. The law further stated that anyone who sought to consider race, religion, color, or nationality in the placement of a child would be considered guilty of a misdemeanor. Between 1924 to 1943, no White child was enrolled in Lincoln Junior High. A suit was brought by two families (the Williams and Hedgepeth families) in 1943 because of the placement of their children at Lincoln Junior High, even though Lincoln was not the closest school to their homes.

Dr. Loser was quoted in the case as saying that it was the "policy of the Board of Education to assign all colored children to The Lincoln School for junior high school work," citing "custom," and an intention to prepare minority groups to "[develop] personally." In 1944, the New Jersey Supreme Court unanimously sided with the Williams and Hedgepeth families against the Trenton School District, rejecting the Loser arguments.

Also in 1944, a group of forward-thinking Trenton leaders, including Roscoe West (President of New Jersey State Teachers College at Trenton, the name of The College at the time), created a community task force, the Trenton Committee for Inter-Racial Unity (later Trenton Committee on Unity). This became a powerful focal point for advocating for change and implementation of integration in Trenton. Despite their impressive work and commitment, in 1947, they reported: "The last time a Negro teacher was employed on a regular (not as a substitute) basis was September 1942." The full report included the fact that at the time, there was only one Black principal out of the twenty-seven in the district. These details became part of the foundation for the change in the New Jersey constitution that banned the denial of civil or military right or segregation in either the military or schools because of "religious principles, race, color, ancestry of national origin." All of these failures in the appointment history were during Dr. Loser's years as superintendent of schools.

In 2016 to 2017, the TCNJ Commission worked hard and carefully digested a lot of material, including the research from the student papers and their own research, holding open fora and soliciting input from on-campus and off-campus constituents, but by late April, with commencement and the summer approaching, there was no formal recommendation from them. I became concerned that the failure to produce the report was being misinterpreted by the community as a delaying tactic. My concerns were reaffirmed by the continuing posting of flyers and a twenty-four-hour sit-in in the president's conference room in Green Hall.

On the morning of April 26, I was in my office meeting with the provost, but I could hear raised voices in the reception area of the president's office. Four students had come to my office demanding to meet with me immediately. They were part of the group of students with whom I had met in December regarding the Loser research. Within five minutes of their leaving the office, there was noise coming from the presidential conference room. The students had found the door to the conference room open and entered. Although I had back-to-back meetings, I went to the conference room to talk to them.

When I entered the conference room, the students were taken aback but immediately shared with me a document with six demands, including the preservation of a mental health clinic run through a department in the School of Education and the changing of the name of Loser Hall. I acknowledged the document and promised to get back to them as soon as possible.

It began with four students.

At 3 p.m., I walked into the conference room and shared with them a written response to their demands. It was a confirming memo summarizing our agreement on a number of issues—that we shared concerns about relationships between The College and Trenton; that the Advisory Commission on Social Justice was named to begin addressing these issues; that The College was working on a number of ways to address the concerns about mental health offerings, including those arising from the closing of the TCNJ Clinic that they sought to preserve. In addition, I agreed that the institution's communication on these plans for mental health offerings had been flawed, and I agreed that on May 4, there would be an information session held on the status of the clinic. I insisted, however, that we describe these as concerns; I would not accept them cast as demands.

By this time, there were at least fifteen students in the room, and lots of pizza boxes (brought in by a friendly faculty member). An hour or so later, I was on my way out the door of the office to attend an event off campus. Heather Fehn called me to her desk outside my office. On her computer monitor, I could see the students in the conference room live streaming to the whole campus.

"Well, yes, she came in to respond to our demands. Well, not respond, actually. She is not going to do anything. She's stonewalling us."

I was furious. I threw my coat to the floor and stormed into the conference room. Heather followed.

By the time I opened the door to the conference area, my inner censor and the support of Heather had toned down my response. Without introduction or request to speak, I said, "What you are saying on the live stream is not only unfair; it is inaccurate. I did, in fact, respond to each point you made in your memo. I told you, however, that I would not accept them as demands; that is not the way members of an academic community interact with one another. You may not like it, but the kind of actions for which you are advocating take time. That's precisely what I have committed to do—to take action but do so in a thoughtful and planful way."

After the encounter, the Vice President of Student Affairs reached out to discuss disciplinary action against the student protesters. While I found the way the students were acting annoying, I thought it would be a huge mistake to escalate the situation by threats of discipline. According to the Student Code of Conduct, refusing to leave a space that is reserved for official purposes required disciplinary action. I pointed out, however, that the president had the authority to determine that action. I concluded that the students would have a statement placed in their disciplinary files indicating that they had been asked to leave the president's conference room and that I had met with them and shared a confirming memo. No other action was to be taken.

By noon on April 27, the students had left the conference room. All the pizza boxes had been gathered and put tidily in large plastic garbage bags. The room looked cleaner than it had before the students arrived. During the twenty-four hours, the students never tried to gain access to my private office, nor the private bathroom attached to the conference suite, but they had made their opinions known.

I asked the co-chairs of the Commission if the recommendation on the name change could be fast-tracked and the other recommendations be included in a follow up report. They agreed.

On May 15, 2017, I announced that I had received a recommendation from the Advisory Commission on Social Justice to remove Dr. Paul Loser's name from the building that housed the Office of Admission and the School of Nursing, Health, and Exercise Science. I found the rationale thoughtful and compelling.

On May 24, 2017, the Board of Trustees received a recommendation from the Executive Committee of the Board of Trustees based on the research and recommendation of the Advisory Commission on Social Justice, Race, and Educational Attainment to President Gitenstein and with her support, that Paul Loser Hall be renamed Trenton Hall, effective immediately. The resolution passed unanimously.

The challenges that confront a president throughout her career are both serendipitous and revelatory, because it is not the crises but the way in which the individual leader reacts that characterizes the way the historical record is kept. The fact that so many of the early crises on the TCNJ campus and the one that was the most volatile (the Loser to Trenton Hall name change) focused on issues of diversity and equity as well as free speech and open inquiry spoke to one of the most torturous but important conundrums in higher education, a conundrum that I placed at the center of my value system. The "endeavoring again" was a constant struggle and a lodestar.

CHAPTER 3

Winter Afternoon Light

There's a certain Slant of light
—**Emily Dickinson**

A ny crisis on a residential campus can become all-consuming, but when there is an overlay of national or international import, the pressure increases. During my presidency, for instance, The College reacted strongly to any number of national political issues, including the election of Barack Obama for his first term and the election of Donald Trump. But none was quite as traumatic or as charged with special power on the campus as 9/11. Part of the reason for that was based on the horrific facts of the events, part of it was peculiar to the location and position of TCNJ. TCNJ is an institution in and of New Jersey. Our students were largely from the state, and many of their families and friends worked in New York City or lived in the New Jersey exurbs of the city, with the World Trade Center as part of their personal skylines.

It was a beautiful, crisp September morning; the sky was that unbelievable blue of fall. I was on my way to a New Jersey Association of State Colleges and Universities (NJASCU) meeting in downtown Trenton. With my meeting material in my briefcase, I picked up my purse and was on my way out the door of my office. Steve Briggs, Provost and Vice President of Academic Affairs, walked into the vestibule of the president's office. He looked stunned when he announced, "A plane has flown into the World Trade Center."

The staff in my office and I were speechless. No one needed to ask which World Trade Center. There was no information about what kind of plane or why the plane flew into the building. Without even thinking, I replied, "It was terrorism."

Why I concluded that, I will never know, but I was absolutely convinced. Strangely enough, I did not even think to question whether I should cancel my appointment. With my purse and briefcase hanging over my right shoulder, I walked to the parking garage where I had parked my car earlier that morning and drove the five miles to Trenton. I parked in the lot behind the NJASCU office and went into the building.

Only a few of my colleagues had arrived. We heard that George Pruitt, President of Thomas Edison State College, whose wife, Pam, worked at the Wall Street Journal Radio station with offices right next to the Trade Center, was not coming. George was glued to the television and working the phones to check on Pam. Susan Cole, President of Montclair State University, eventually made it into the NJASCU office. Her face was ashen.

"I was in my car on the New Jersey turnpike. My driver said, 'Look! Oh my God.' I looked over my shoulder and I could see it—the smoke and flames from the building. I think I saw the second plane hit the South tower. I am not really sure."

I had never seen Susan flustered. Clearly, there was not going to be a meeting today, so I left the office to find Don, who worked in an office nearby. He and I tried to get some news on his computer and then I realized that I had to get back to the campus. It was only 10:30 a.m. By the time I returned to my office, the horror was becoming more apparent, and I did what I often do at such times: I shifted into crisis mode.

I turned to my assistants and made an outrageous request: We needed to figure out just how many from our community could have experienced personal impact from this disaster. We needed to contact Student Affairs, Business, and Finance, all the deans' offices, Provost Office, and Human Resources. We needed to get a sense of just how many students lived in the New Jersey towns nearest lower Manhattan. We needed to reach out to networks of students to see if they could help collect anecdotal evidence of who might have had family who could have been working at the Trade Center or nearby. We needed to do the same for faculty and staff.

I do not know why I thought that information was necessary or even useful, but I did. Perhaps it would provide some sense of reality to such an unbelievable event. Within two and a half hours, we had a guesstimate that at least 2,000 students, faculty, or staff could have had a close relation in the explosion. I sent an email out to the cabinet and asked them to share the message with their senior staff: "I want none of you sitting in your offices today. Everyone should be out and about on the campus. Students, faculty, and staff should see us. Take the initiative to guide people to support services. Be seen."

By mid-day, I sent an email to the community urging everyone to be present for one another, to be together with others, with friends, to stay away from solitary watching of the news reports. I made sure that large screen TVs were available in dining halls and that all eating venue hours were extended. Like everyone else, we optimistically called for people to make blood donations. Students scheduled a gathering for 3:30 p.m. that afternoon. I reminded everyone in my remarks that we still did not know the facts and that we should withhold judgment, but that we should be sending love to those who had lost loved ones. In the days that followed, both Provost Briggs and I continued our frequent communication with the community.

On Friday, we held a memorial service in our largest formal space, Kendall Hall. It was packed. It was fortunate that we had decided to live stream the ceremony, so that those who could not fit into the auditorium could participate. Probably half of the almost 8,500-person community (7,500 students and 1,000 faculty and staff) were watching in venues all over the campus—in the student center and in the public areas in residence halls.

Representatives from all religious organizations joined me, the chairman of the board, and student leadership to mourn those we thought had died, the families who were suffering in their lack of knowledge, and the country that had lost its innocence. I ended my remarks with words of Dickinson as she describes that special winter light that both oppresses and memorializes, that makes us pause in our regular life, and that finally allows us to let go of the dead.

Within days, we had confirmed that parents of two current students had been in or near the site at the time of the attacks: Kristine Benson and Christopher Ludwig. Like most who felt the personal brunt of that terrible day, the families and the TCNJ community did not know the fate of Mrs. Benson or Mr. Ludwig. For the longest time, the Bensons were "hospital hopping," trying to find any news about Kristine's mother, who worked for the New Jersey Port Authority. On October 30, almost two months later, there was a funeral for Margaret L. Benson; faculty from the History Department attended to represent TCNJ. Like most who died in the Towers, the bodies of neither of these parents were ever found, but there was confirmation of their presence in the Towers when the explosions destroyed the buildings.

These delayed losses and the pall that covered our lives weighted every moment during those weeks. We were never able to ascertain the exact number of alumni or family members who died in the Twin Towers collapse, but the centrality of the event to the life of The College is clear in the number of initiatives to provide support for victims and their families by offices and departments across the campus. Alumni and members of the TCNJ community exhibited incredible dedication and love. The spring 2002 issue of *The College of New Jersey: EMagazine* included examples of heroic alumni who worked on a "mass casualty truck" and the pile; those who worked on rescue squads; and those who died in the tower collapse. It's hard to recapture those times, but there is no one who lived through them that will forget the horror of what we knew and what we did not know.

On September 11, 2002, Chris Ludwig, whose father, Lee Charles Ludwig, died in the Twin Towers, spoke at a service commemorating the one-year anniversary of the tragedy. Chris was remarkably composed, and his words were beautiful.

"Four years ago, my father got a better job that moved him out of a beige, plain, and forgettable thirty-six-story building on Wall Street, over a few blocks to Church Street and Vesey, and up another ninety stories in the air into that shining silver tower at World Trade 2." If that promotion had not occurred, perhaps his father would have come back home on September 11, 2001. Chris saw his job on that anniversary as not to make sense of that day for others, but just to make sense of it for himself. That combination of uniqueness with shared loss captured the feel for anyone touched by 9/11.

The distinct horror of 9/11 on the TCNJ and Central Jersey community was exacerbated by the fact that within a month of the attacks, anthrax was reported to have been found in the post office facility in nearby Hamilton Township. The sense of vulnerability and fear transformed us even further.

In October, the *New York Times* invited a group of female university and college presidents to join them in the newspaper offices to discuss how we had reacted and handled the terrorist attacks. There were about twenty of us from all over the country; three were from either New York or the New York metropolitan area. When it came time to describe our experiences, it was clear that the experience of the three of us from New York and New Jersey was different from that of others across the nation. No doubt 9/11 was a national disaster and there were more sites than the World Trade Center. But the scope of the loss was more visceral for us: the weeks of watching local news about "working on the pile," stories of families "hospital hopping," the stories of anguished emergency room staff waiting for victims that never arrived. That local focus, like the *New York Times* itself, made it very personal.

One of my colleagues, Marlene Springer, who was then president of the College of Staten Island, an institution that catered to "non-traditional" students, many of whom were seeking credentials to improve a career, said at one point in the *Times* meeting that she never remembered hugging so many middle-aged fire fighters as they wept about the loss of colleagues and family members.

After 9/11, our sense of safety on the campus was shaken, and then after the horror and aftermath of a student death in 2006 (discussed in Chapter 4), I came to understand that we did not live in some idyllic world, protected from the threats of the outside. It was necessary that we upgrade and professionalize the police department. In 2008, we conducted a thorough review of our security office on campus, creating a service that included sworn police officers, security officers, and public safety communications experts, led by a sworn police chief. We hired John Collins as Chief of Police. Chief Collins came to TCNJ from the Port Authority of New York and New Jersey, having served as the commanding officer of the Lincoln Tunnel, during the months following the Towers' collapse.

When Collins retired in 2017, TCNJ had established well-developed protocols for managing critical incidents with clearly delineated roles and responsibilities for police, staff, and administration. There were regularly scheduled drills for possible crises on a campus, including active shooter drills and drills for more likely events, such as chemical spills and fires. I learned to depend on him and his wisdom in managing crisis and to understand my position in times of crisis, but I could only do so if I had total confidence in those responsible for safety and security of the campus.

The first time I really appreciated that change—not only in the professionalism of the police services on the campus, but also in my confidence in that professionalism—was as the crowd was gathering for the annual 2012 President's Toast for the Senior Class at the fountain in the Science Complex. The students were festively dressed for the dinner dance to follow; I was walking around talking to them and wishing them well. Out of the corner of my eye, I saw a man acting strangely, seeming to search behind each tree. My pulse became elevated. I began to follow him to figure out what he was doing. Then I saw Chief Collins. He and Captain Grant were following the man, finally walking up to him. I overheard as he said, "Oh, yeah, I am the sound guy, looking to make sure the speakers work."

I learned two things that night—one, I was not a good snoop, and two, there were those on the staff at TCNJ who were.

Outreach from colleagues and friends was lifesaving during the weeks and months after 9/11. Clayton Brower, president of The College from 1971 to 1979, was in touch with me from the beginning of my tenure as president. I will never forget how his first email response to the series of racist and antisemitic graffiti gave me courage. He'd seen a copy of our student newspaper and wanted to tell me what a good job I was doing. Only he could have reassured me that way.

After 9/11, when Clayt had heard of the memorial service and the way we had sought to reassure the campus community after the anthrax story, he again reached out. He was the best example of what a previous president can do to help support a successor. I will always consider his kindness and wisdom as important reasons why I succeeded in the job.

While less dramatic, managing campus reaction to national presidential politics is also not simple. There were three moments that serve as examples of where I aimed to craft institutional messaging to the central purposes of higher education and The College's mission, not to partisan politics.

The first was when Barack Obama was elected President of the United States in 2008. The students, particularly the Black students, were electrified. Across the nation and on the TCNJ campus, college-aged students took credit for the victory. There was a palpable feeling on the campus of a generation mobilized and celebratory in their victory. I was concerned about seeming partisan in any institutional response, but then I concluded that this was not a partisan issue, but rather a transformative moment in the history of our country. A new generation was taking leadership in national politics; the first African

American had been elected to the highest office in the land. I remember hearing from my closest professional friend in the ranks of presidential leadership in New Jersey, George Pruitt, who is African American. "If Obama gets elected, I will simply have to take a day. This will be momentous. I never thought I would see the day."

Working with the Vice President of Student Affairs and the leadership in academic affairs, we arranged for the open space in the Student Center to be transformed so that students could watch the inauguration of America's first Black president. While there were viewing opportunities in classrooms and in the dining hall, Eickhoff Hall, the atmosphere in Brower Student Center was exhilarating. The audience was racially mixed and all groups on the campus were represented—students, faculty, administration, and staff. Indeed, the most joyous of the group were the custodians and other facilities staff who believed that Obama's election proved that we had entered a new era in our country.

Donald Trump's election as President of the United States was a second moment in time where national politics had tremendous impact on the campus climate. His election was not just a shock to the system for the community, it was also an important lesson in the process of democracy and historical trends. I cannot remember how many times I had to respond to students who said in 2016, "Well, Trump's not my president." To each one of them I responded, "Actually, he is our president, and we must deal with that." Student reaction on the campus was immediate and visceral; many felt that this was a rebuke of all that they had done to chart a new direction. Some parents were understanding, but many others were critical of any actions we took to support students in this transition. About a week after the election, the School of Humanities and Social Sciences sponsored a program that was intended as a platform for students to process the results of the 2016 election. The general campus email was co-signed by the Provost and the Vice President of Student Affairs.

Vice President Hecht received an irate phone call from a parent accusing us of coddling students. She believed that her daughter, a Trump voter, would be targeted by others. She wanted the event canceled. In her opinion, it was not our job to teach students about respect. She threatened that if she did not receive a call back before the event, she would not only call the governor's office, but she would also show up on campus. This same mother, who refused to give either her last name or her daughter's name, also called my office. The Humanities and Social Science event was held, that mother did not show up on campus, the governor never called TCNJ regarding the election, but none of this stopped others from reaching out to my office regarding their concerns, disapproval of our response, and similar threats.

Not all the objections were so intolerant. I received some thoughtful objections from students. One upperclassman wrote in an email that he thought the only reason for the institutional messages and programming was because Trump rather than Clinton had been elected. He felt as though we were not trying to bring students together. He felt the institutional response was premature and disrespectful not only to the students but also to democracy. He asserted that there were many students who felt silenced by the emails. He said that he objected to some of what Donald Trump said, but he also objected to the conclusion that because he voted for Trump, he was a bigot. In my response, I not only thanked him for his candid and thoughtful response but urged him to share any information about targeted attacks on community members with appropriate administrative offices.

Another student wrote an even more compelling and considered objection. He cited my words from my opening address. I had argued that we had to approach difficult discussions with an open mind. He asserted, however, that what the administration was doing was contradictory to the open mind I had called for in my opening speech. In his opinion, the faculty and administration were encouraging the divisiveness they so strongly criticized. Both individuals highlighted the feeling that Republicans were afraid to speak up on campus.

I concluded that whatever we in the TCNJ administration asserted, we were not fostering an opportunity for open discussion. While unintentional, we were perpetuating the shutdown of discussion that many were fearing from the incoming national leadership. Partnering with academic and student affairs professionals, we began a process of creating a more balanced foundation for conversation. We engaged with Sustained Dialogues, an organization based in Washington, D.C. that helped communities develop skills to reach across lines of disagreement to develop understanding and respect. The topics for these conversations in its first offerings included "Post Inauguration," "Invisible Inequality: Social Class," "Balancing a Culture of Excellence," and "Bridging Difference: Understanding Racial Interactions." Each had a faculty and a student facilitator. One of our most involved student leaders in this endeavor was the student who cited my opening speech as the platform for his criticism of what the faculty and administration were doing on the campus. His participation and leadership were instrumental in broadening and leavening our discussions.

President Trump's stance specifically on immigration in general and Deferred Action for Childhood Arrivals (DACA) students in particular was a third moment in which national politics had a significant impact on the life of TCNJ and my public statements as president of The College of New Jersey. On January 27, 2017, President Trump announced an Executive Order which suspended all immigration to the United States from Iran, Iraq, Libya, Somalia, Sudan, Syria, and Yemen. A week later, I sent out a public statement objecting to the action. I aligned my objections to the statement by the American Association of State Colleges and Universities (AASCU) and to my joining with more than 600 other presidents of institutions of higher education urging the federal government to reconsider its position on DACA. While I emphasized that all information about national origin of students or employees at TCNJ was private and would not be shared without a valid subpoena or court order, I urged anyone who was from one of these countries to avoid foreign travel until they received legal advice. I felt strongly that it was appropriate for me to feel and to express a particular obligation to the DACA students.

While there was a good feeling of shared purpose in aligning myself with the DACA advocacy, there was little evidence that it was effective. In fact, on September 5, 2017, the Trump administration announced its intent to "wind down" the DACA program. I still felt my voice needed to be raised on this issue not just on campus, but beyond. I was a member of the Executive Committee of the New Jersey State Chamber of Commerce. I reached out to that body to ask the Chamber to consider endorsing DACA. I couched the request as a good business decision for contributing members of the society, indicating that since the Trump announcement, more than 400 CEOs including those from Microsoft, Amazon, Google, Hewlett-Packard, Lyft, Netflix, Twitter, Facebook, Verizon, IBM, Uber, and Y Combinator expressed support for DACA. On September 5, the US Chamber of Commerce had done the same. The New Jersey Chamber followed suit at its October 3, 2017 meeting.

At TCNJ, we took specific actions to provide support services for students who self-identified as DACA, including legal resources from local law schools, facilitation by TCNJ administrators to identify pro bono legal advice from volunteer lawyers, and transportation to information sessions that were held at nearby New Jersey law schools.

Looking back, I believe that all these actions were in keeping with The College's mission and my principles of speaking out and taking action on issues that were central to institutional mission. The decision to celebrate Obama's historic election was perhaps a bit too close to partisanship. The response to the 2016 election was a work in progress for several weeks, and I believe that we wisely redirected our rhetoric and programming in the face of legitimate student concerns. By engaging thoughtful students with contrary opinions in the process of Sustained Dialogues, we accomplished much of the charge I had given to the community in my Welcome Back address: "to come together and support each other all the while respecting the diverse viewpoints we have on campus." The advocacy for DACA, while not as effective as I had hoped, was central to my advocacy for fairness in higher education and garnered the most external support.

In the cases where we were successful in engaging the community well in understanding actions and events of national and international import, I believe that we were able to incorporate thoughtful disagreement. We were able to listen to one another, acknowledging the shadows holding their breaths around us as well as the true life and death import of what we were confronting.

CHAPTER 4

Loss Again

Burglar! Banker—Father!
I am poor once more!

—Emily Dickinson

Having a real affection and admiration for the students of an institution is perhaps the most important reason for accepting the difficult job of president of an institution of higher education. At a largely undergraduate, primarily residential campus, the president must acknowledge, however, that this tie can be volatile, and student reactions to administrative decisions and to student-based crises can become problematic.

Sometimes, there are strong reactions to what would seem a minor administrative decision. For instance, in the spring of 2003, TCNJ undertook a review of the logo for The College. The image of a cupola atop the iconic Green Hall was generic; it looked like logos from a hundred other colleges and a thousand high schools across the nation. While the conclusion to develop a more distinctive logo was well founded, the process for doing so was ill-conceived. There was little outreach to student, faculty, or alumni representatives to seek input.

Within hours of the announcement of the new, streamlined alphabetic TCNJ shield logo, a petition objecting to the change was launched, which received approximately 2,000 signatures, some of which came with strong language beside their objections. A senior biology major wrote me a thoughtful letter about her concerns. She began with compliments about my leadership and thanked me as a model for female students, but then expressed both her concerns about the lack of consultation and the quality of the logo as well as her unhappiness with the nastiness of some of the comments on the petition. The maturity of her communication reinforced my growing discomfort with the process we had used.

Not everyone who objected was as polite or considerate as the biology major. During April 2003, there were a number of articles in the *Signal*, almost all of which were negative about the process and the result; there were protests at the campus Task Force meeting on institutional identity. One of the loudest critics of the institutional name change in 1996, Joe Ellis, Professor of History, saw the initiative as another attempt to separate The College from its history. The *Signal* quoted him as saying, "Why do we give a damn what we look like nationally? This isn't an Ivy League college. This isn't an Ivy League anything."

There was some pointed criticism about spending money on any marketing initiative in the context of threatened budget cuts. There were snide observations about the new logo's apparent similarity to the logo of Princeton University. Most of the criticism by students, faculty, and alumni, however, was about the fact that there was little to no consultation or involvement of the community in the planning.

I believed then and I believe now that the shield logo was much superior to the cupola one, because it was more distinctive, but the process for developing that logo was flawed. This was a self-inflicted wound that required much administrative time in response. In the end, the process had a negative impact on what should have been a positive decision. In 2014, when The College engaged a marketing firm to help us with a revisioning of the institutional brand, the process was entirely different. There was significant outreach to all stakeholder groups. When the announcement of the new brand was made, there were some objections to that new branding initiative; however, the preponderance of the reactions for the new standards was supportive.

As problematic as these kinds of student and faculty objections to administrative actions could be, nothing could compare to the real times of crisis on a campus, like the ones described in Chapter 3. No crisis can compare to the aftereffects of a student death. Perhaps the hardest times for a president of an institution with a large population of eighteen to twenty-two-year-olds are those times when one of your students dies, particularly if that death is by suicide. During my years at TCNJ, there were five confirmed student suicides. There were a number of other student deaths, at least one of which was a suspected suicide. While each one of these deaths was as hard as the first and each time provided its own specific set of facts, I approached each with a certain basic set of principles.

When I was Chairman of the English Department at SUNY-Oswego, I had learned the hard lessons of the importance of communication in the immediate aftermath of a community death, when in 1986, a faculty member shot himself. Advice on communication in such tragedies was not as accessible then as it is now, but I was fortunate to receive exceptional advice from Rabbi Sheldon Ezrig, the rabbi of Temple Concord in Syracuse, New York, the congregation to which I belonged at the time. The rabbi had training in crisis management, particularly communication on the heels of death by suicide. He counseled to avoid euphemisms, use words like "suicide" and "death," always be seen, and always be present. Such communication requires almost brutal honesty and providing emotional support to both students and faculty as they process the loss.

I took the rabbi's advice seriously in that instance and in every similar circumstance during my life as an administrator. Every time there was a death, and I was in a position of leadership, I knew that honesty, availability, and presence were essential. I used the words "suicide" and "death," and I avoided euphemisms. I was present at memorial services. I reached out personally to the family of the student. But every time the appointed hour came, I dreaded the phone call. What was I to say? Almost every time I called, I realized that it was not the words that mattered, it was the simple fact of the call.

After my outreach, some of the parents wrote in appreciation. After one such death from injuries suffered from a suicide attempt the month before, the family wrote, "The support and kindness you have shown toward our family during this difficult time will always be remembered. We cannot thank you enough for the many things that you did to help our family while we stayed with [our son] . . . It just conveys to us once again what a supportive and caring community [he] was a part of at TCNJ and our daughter . . . is still part of as she looks forward to her senior year. Your consideration and thoughtfulness have helped us get through these challenging days and those still to come."

Every single one of these losses devastated the community. I took every one of them to heart. But the one that upended the campus most traumatically was the case of George Smith in spring of 2006. While I would not know until the next day, according to the police report, George, a freshman, returned to his residence hall early Saturday morning, March 25, and was last seen at 3 a.m. asleep on a friend's floor. On March 27, everyone was looking toward 2 p.m., the time of his first class, hoping that George would show up for class. When he did not, the state police were called in as investigators.

At the beginning of that week in March, my focus had been on two critical problems before The College—an almost 32 percent cut in state funding for higher education in Governor Corzine's budget proposal, and a troubled construction project that eventually required legal action by the institution to throw the construction company off the campus. By the end of that week, all my attention was on finding George Smith.

March 29 was the beginning of the circus that destroyed any semblance of normalcy on the TCNJ campus for the spring 2006 semester. By 9 a.m., there were police and media helicopters hovering over the campus; there were wild rumors flying across campus, including one that George's body had been found in the dumpster behind his residence hall. In order to mitigate the rampant speculations that naturally grow in times of crisis, we began a practice of at least daily email updates for the community, emails in which we shared the facts as we knew them.

Our effort at transparency did nothing to keep the less scrupulous of the press from speculating recklessly, nor from their invading the personal space and sense of safety of our students. Over the next two weeks, we experienced the underbelly of the twenty-four-hour news cycle. On a local radio station, 101.5 (not the campus station), TCNJ was topic number one on their afternoon broadcasts. Because there had been a tragic and sudden campus death in the fall, the Jersey Guys (on-air personalities known for their sensationalistic reporting) began to refer to TCNJ as Death U.

Several staff and students succumbed to the temptation to call in their objections to the way The College was being described. Their words did nothing to mitigate the 101.5 coverage. The campus was suffering from the facts that were known, the rampant speculations, and the overriding goal of the press to keep the story alive without any regard to the feelings of those closest to the student. Throughout it all, there was the sound of hovering helicopters.

The mass email communication with the campus was supplemented with a series of face-to-face meetings that I had with the Student Government Association, the Faculty Senate, the Staff Senate, and the campus-wide planning committee (Committee on Strategic Planning and Priorities). I was insistent on communicating what we knew with compassion and accuracy and doing so face to face when possible. There were no public appearances that I made in the following several weeks at which I did not specifically reference the case. I answered all questions with facts as I knew them. I did not speculate on causes. I admitted when I either did not know something or could not reveal details that needed to remain confidential for the integrity of the investigation.

It had only been four days since George had been reported missing, but it felt as if months had passed. Then, unbelievably, another student was reported missing. While we had information that led us to believe that more than likely, the young woman had simply left town with no notification, we concluded that it would be better for us to share the information of her disappearance. The fearful and the sensation seekers found this additional missing student grist for even more emotional anxiety. Within two days, it was confirmed that the female student had bought an airline ticket to Miami and had been found by Miami police.

The decision to share the information of her going missing, even in the midst of our concerns about George, served us well. While the good news of the second student being found did not dampen the efforts to stir up hysteria, the students and parents who were looking to the administration for confirmation that the students and their well-being were at the center of our thoughts were reassured. We were willing to share information even if the result could be negative publicity. They could trust us. I was gratified that students recognized that I had kept them front and center in my concerns over George's death. Early in the summer, a 2006 graduate wrote, "As you said at graduation, this has been a difficult year for all of us at TCNJ. But you have led our school with grace and commitment, and I thank you."

Since I had decided to forego an alumni trip to Florida, I took time to record a video greeting that was to be shared with the alumni who attended the event. As I sat before the video camera, a part-time staff member took the opportunity to pass on his theories on the Smith case. Had we thought of searching the ponds on campus? Had we thought of checking on missing patients from the local psychiatric hospital? This conversation was repeated innumerable times over the next four months. For those with good intentions (like this man), they simply could not believe that the solution was not just around the corner. This kind of horror did not happen on our campus, in our community. The fear of a lengthy period or a forever of not knowing the facts was overwhelming.

I was receiving many emails from parents, most of whom were

appreciative of the information we were sharing with both their students and them (through the parent listserv). However, I was also beginning to hear complaints about the aggressive intrusion of the press into the students' personal lives. While we continued to believe that George's was not a story of inadequate on-campus security, we realized that we had to take some public action to help mitigate the fears of parents and students. We finally concluded that we would have to "lock down" the residence halls.

We simply could not protect our students from the press. To my dismay, even that decision to lock down the halls did not protect the students. The day we implemented the changes for entry to residence halls, a student worker in my office who lived in Travers-Wolfe (the freshman residence halls) called to ask for advice. He had been accosted by a reporter (who had slipped into the hall by pretending to be a student). The reporter thrust a mic in front of the student's face and said, "I hear you work in the president's office; do you have something special to share with me?"

While most of the emails and communications from parents were reasonable and supportive, there were some who were quick to attack campus policies and procedures and to demand changes in security. The fact that all the police and security agencies had deemed the campus safe and secure was not convincing to these parents. We were judged to be a safe campus according to federal guidelines. In compliance with the Clery Act, higher education institutions are required to release an Annual Security Report providing statistics on campus crime. Year after year, TCNJ's report documented the low levels of crime on the campus. But the statistics could not stand up to the power of the media frenzy.

It is understandable that in the fear of the moment, parents seek assurance of absolute safety, an ideal that no one, not even the parents themselves, can promise their children no matter where they live. These parental communications ranged from those who were just scared and concerned to the most aggressive behaviors of "helicopter" parents, including offering themselves as sources to the media who were seeking to sensationalize the story. What we sought to do at the institutional level was to be transparent, open, and responsive.

Pressure was mounting on the authorities to make a public statement. The state police and the prosecutor's office finally agreed to a press conference to confirm what had already been widely reported: A significant amount of blood had been found in the dumpster behind George's residence hall. With the help of biological samples from George's parents, the blood had been positively identified as an offspring of the Smiths. It was George's blood. The emotional landscape on the day of that press conference was surreal.

At the press conference, there were three scheduled speakers: the prosecutor, a representative of the state police, and me. I had gained a tremendous amount of respect for the state police throughout the week, but my admiration and appreciation grew significantly during and after this press conference. Throughout, they were professional and sensitive to the nature of the campus community and the probable horrific outcome. The prosecutor, on the other hand, sometimes appeared insensitive to the pain of the circumstance, willingly answering questions regarding the mechanics of the trash compacting system on the campus, which left many of the students in attendance either in stunned silence or collapsed in tears. On the evening news and in the next day's print press, the reporters pushed hard on the authorities, but they acknowledged the campus shock and pain. We received much media attention in the local and regional press, hitting both the Philadelphia and New York City media markets. This was not the kind of media attention I would have sought.

We were fortunate that the waste management company we used had a sophisticated Global Positioning System, the records of which could track not just which truck picked up the trash from Travers-Wolfe on March 27, but also at which landfill that load of trash would have been deposited. On April 1, the search began at a Tulleytown, Pennsylvania landfill (approximately ten miles from campus). To see the daily videos of the search in the landfill was deeply painful, but at least it removed the campus from the television lens—if only for a short while.

We recognized that the details of the news conference would be top of mind for anyone still deciding on accepting admission to TCNJ in the fall. We decided that we would have to hold a strategy session on how we would manage our planned Accepted Students Day (The College's largest admissions event), scheduled for the weekend after the press conference. We concluded that we would hold the day as planned, that in keeping with our philosophy of the value of transparency, we would add three opportunities for parents and potential students to meet with me, Interim Vice President for Student Life Beth Paul, and Associate Vice President Kathryn Leverton for Facilities and Administration to discuss security. We were prepared to answer questions about the Smith case and the impact of the governor's budget proposal.

The three sessions with parents held during our Accepted Students Day were reasonably well-attended. I was pleased that two trustees were present in the audience to show support for the campus and administration. It seemed particularly noteworthy that they were both alumnae, a reaffirmation of the wisdom of my goal to increase the percentage of alumni serving as trustees. Most of the parents at the sessions and those who were interviewed by local media seemed to be convinced that TCNJ was, in fact, a safe campus and that we had been forthright regarding the facts surrounding the case.

Many of the questions regarding safety were those that trouble all parents as they face the stress of letting go of their students. The questions at the sessions I attended were not focused on any specifics regarding George's disappearance or even on concerns about student behavior in general. The most frequent question was about the size of bed sheets. We, however, felt that it was important to be frank and responsive, sharing information that the parents might not even know to ask about. We openly talked of our strategies to combat prevalent kinds of destructive student behavior, such as alcohol abuse, that was much in the news. We also spoke of our partnership with the authorities in seeking answers to George's disappearance.

Cards, calls, and emails throughout the week from friends of TCNJ were revealing. The most important messages I got were ones that simply expressed sympathy and concern. They came from a wide range of individuals—former board members, personal friends, family members, professional colleagues, business leaders, alumni, students, parents, and a couple of politicians. I was touched by a letter from Jim Brazell, a professor emeritus at TCNJ and stepfather of a former student who died tragically in a car crash only three years earlier. He and his wife, Kathy, remarked on my "passionate attachment to the school and its students." One of the most meaningful calls came from our state assemblywoman, Bonnie Watson-Coleman, who was also the state Democratic party chair. She called not so much as a politician but rather as a woman and mother.

A couple of our students had an eye-opening experience by agreeing to be interviewed on the Nancy Grace show on CNN in early April. The students were up against a full range of supposed experts who were blissfully uninformed of the specifics of the investigation of the George Smith case and absolutely confident of their conclusions. The version of the "experts" was that George had been murdered. They were convinced that the authorities knew this fact and that we were covering up a murder. The experts could provide no evidence for their conclusions, but that failure in no way moderated the certitude of their tone. The students tried to provide the facts of the relative safety of the campus and the supportiveness and openness of the administration, but the experts knew better. Like the previous experience with the local radio station, the only positive that came for our students was learning to be circumspect in engaging with voices who were more interested in ratings than accuracy.

I received several offers from public relations firms for consulting services to help us message about the crisis. I declined them all, turning instead to Matt Golden, the talented administrator responsible for communications. Matt's sensitivity to the campus culture was flawless, his advice on tone and manner impeccable. The success of our communications plans regarding the Smith crisis was largely because of his extraordinary talent.

While the board at TCNJ was supportive of me throughout the dual crises at The College (the student disappearance and the state budget proposal), particularly in the new era of concern about board accountability, they also had to be clear in their communication with the public about their own responsibilities and accountabilities. As the months extended, most of the board became concerned about the burden on me and reached out to me in kind ways. I deeply appreciated these individual expressions of personal support, but what I came to appreciate was that managing the combined crises was not the board's responsibility—it was mine, and frankly, no one could lessen the burden or pressure for me as president. There were members of the executive staff and, of course, Don, who bolstered my emotional health, but even they could not take this burden from me.

This period of time was one when I knew that canard about seeking work-life balance was ridiculous. I felt the pressure tremendously, but I also welcomed the responsibility because I cared so deeply about the community and wanted to help lead it through this difficult time. My appreciation of this responsibility stood me in good stead to stem some trustee inclinations of becoming too involved in management issues on the campus.

Even though there was no closure on the Smith case, there was a growing feeling on the campus that the students needed some kind of formal event to honor George. The student religious groups organized a prayer service in George's honor. As the time for the memorial approached, there was press outside the Spiritual Center, at a respectful distance, but still hovering in the background. To my surprise, George's father appeared at the service with his sister. He looked haunted, much worse than in any photos or videos that I had previously seen. The service was strained, not only because of Mr. Smith's presence, but because of the deep sadness about George's loss that permeated the campus. In order to avoid the press, when we left, I asked the campus police to escort me and Beth Paul to our cars.

In mid-April, a group of college and university presidents from

Mercer County (the county in which TCNJ is situated) met with the editorial board of one of the local newspapers, the *Trentonian*. The meeting went well and resulted in a positive article and editorial regarding restoration of funds for higher education. But in the spring of 2006, the story of George Smith was never far away.

Paul Mickel, one of the reporters, asked for a private conversation with me as the presidents prepared to leave. He acknowledged the tremendous difficulty for TCNJ over the last couple of months and insisted that he would always be fair in reporting, but then he said, "I just want to let you know that I will never ever let go of the George Smith story. I cannot believe that this is a simple story of accidental death. The kid and his parents deserve more."

Perhaps I should have been surprised, and certainly, I should have been more circumspect; after all, this was a news reporter of a local newspaper who could easily write whatever he wanted, a newspaper that took seriously the adage, "if it bleeds it leads," but I was furious.

"Surely, you do not mean to imply that your upset or concern is greater than mine. Let me assure you, other than George's family and close friends, no one is more concerned or disturbed by his disappearance than I."

I was again reminded that I was not going to be able to focus solely on the budget crisis or on the goal of leading the campus through the Smith horror. In both cases, everyone from editors to politicians was anxious to provide the simple answer to the complex and intractable problems before us. There were those who proposed another cut to our already decimated administrative and staff personnel to solve the extraordinary budget crisis of a 32 percent possible cut to state funding, and there were those who firmly believed that more publicity would lead to a student confessing involvement in George's disappearance. The trick for me was to balance an openness to positive input with my natural impatience for those who were unwilling, or in some cases, unable to realize the complexity of the problems we faced, while at the same time acknowledging that such simple actions would not address these complex problems.

While recognizing that he might not be able to provide me a great deal of additional information, I requested and was able to schedule a meeting with the lead investigator from the state police, a talented and focused young man, almost frightening in his intensity. Unfortunately, what he shared with me reinforced my concern that we would perhaps never know exactly what happened to George Smith. The investigator suggested that the authorities felt good about where they were looking for the body. He asserted that he found no evidence that anyone was hiding information that would reveal the specifics of the early morning hours of March 25. I left the meeting with more questions than answers surrounding the fact of George's blood in the trash receptacle.

Public institutions in New Jersey are required to hold an annual public hearing to present plans for any increase in tuition or fees. We were always careful to present alternative scenarios, dependent on our speculations on what the July 1 legislative budget would be. We included detailed explanations for increases and plans for where the additional revenue would be expended.

The day before that hearing, a body was found in the Tulleytown landfill. As the hearing began on April 26, Matt Golden informed me that he had received a phone call with the information about the discovery of the body. While there was not yet confirmation that this was George's body, all indications were that it was. Apparently, the reporter in the audience at the hearing from the *Trenton Times* had received a similar phone call, and consequently, he stopped me as I left the room to inquire what I knew. While I declined to confirm or deny any report, I said that, assuming that George was deceased, finding the body would be a good thing. It would be what we had been looking for over the last three weeks.

On that same day, a press conference was held confirming the body found was that of George Smith. Before the press conference, in a private briefing for senior TCNJ administration, the lead investigator shared a description of the body after three weeks in a landfill and the transport through the waste management system.

"Stop," I said. "I guess that some in this room need to know these details, but no one outside this room does. I am the mother of this campus, and I see absolutely no reason for my students to have to hear these horrific details shared in public this afternoon. Surely, you will have to share them with the press at some point. But not now, and not on my campus. I watched how students crumbled in tears last time when we went through the details of the trash compacting system. Not again."

After the press conference, I walked around campus to see and be seen by students. I was walking toward a reporter, when a student saw me and came up to me to thank me for how I had handled the horrible events surrounding George's death, to thank me particularly for how I had provided support for the students on George's residence hall floor. After thanking the student, clearly within earshot, the reporter greeted me and asked my opinion on the how and why of George's death. I politely refused to answer these questions and instead spoke of the impact of the loss on the entire campus. Then, a faculty member, also within earshot of the reporter, stopped me to share his compliments on the institution's handling of the Smith tragedy.

I read the reporter's newspaper the next day and found exactly what I expected: no reference to either of these interactions or any quotation from the president of TCNJ. The reporter had a story to tell, and he was going to report evidence for what he had expected to find. The story had to focus on the mystery, the most damaging speculations, the assumption that the campus distrusted the administration. If interactions did not support that narrative, they need not be included.

Once the news of the identification of George's body was public knowledge, and after confirming with the family liaison on the next day that the Smiths would accept my call, I called their home. While I always made these calls, I knew this one would be especially difficult. Mrs. Smith answered the phone sounding guarded. After expressing my condolences, I shared with her that the next day, a group of George's friends were planning to plant a tree in her son's honor, that Beth Paul, Interim Vice President of Student Affairs, who was in the room with me at the time, would call back with specifics.

In addition, as in other cases of a student death, I requested that if she shared with us specifics about their funeral plans, we would share that with George's college friends. I also shared that when and if they were interested in an additional service on campus, we would work with them for such. Whatever the cause—Mrs. Smith's tone, or my deep regret that the reported preference of the family delayed my outreach to them—this was the most painful condolence call to a parent I ever made. I hung up the phone, shaking uncontrollably. I was relieved that Beth was in the office to help me sit down. At 1 p.m. on Friday, April 28, a simple and heartfelt program was scheduled for the planting of the hope tree for George. Mrs. Smith attended.

In late May, the family held a memorial service for their son in Mantua, New Jersey. Beth Paul attended the service, as did George's roommate and several of his floormates from Wolfe Four. Reports of the service were heartbreaking. It was reported in the *Philadelphia Inquirer* that George's father admitted that he had had a history of misuse of alcohol and that his son had begun drinking at college. In the *Trenton Times*, alcoholism was attributed to George himself and both the *Inquirer* and the *Times* reported that the students who had last seen George on March 25 described him as drunk.

On June 5, the day after the reports of the memorial service, we received notification of the Smiths' intent to file a claim against The College of New Jersey, accusing the institution of negligence, particularly with regard to failure to enforce our alcohol policy. Such a claim would need to establish negligence or willing disregard that led to George's death, or it would need to establish that the institution had failed to take some action to prevent that death or withheld information about the death. None of this was true, but the death was so devastating and horrific that it was not surprising that the family would file such a claim.

Because TCNJ, as a component unit of the state of New Jersey, is not a "sue or be sued" entity, the case would be against the state of New Jersey. Should such a suit go forward, the New Jersey Treasury's Division of Risk Management and the State Attorney General's Office, not TCNJ, would evaluate appropriate action and response under the New Jersey Tort Claims Act. Six years after the first notice, the State settled a civil suit brought by the family with no finding or admission of wrongdoing by TCNJ, and without any finding of the cause of George's death.

No doubt the fact that there was no certitude about what led to George's death added to the distress of family, friends, and other members of the TCNJ community. George was a well-liked, healthy young man. How could he die without any explanation? It seemed so irrational and unfair. This kind of cognitive dissonance leads some people to seek a more rational answer. Someone or some entity must be at fault. While I do not know what led to George's death, I firmly believe that The College could not have foreseen or prevented his death. The support services for students during this time period were exemplary and the investigation of George's disappearance was extensive.

The residential program at TCNJ is well-known nationally for its developmental focus on student growth, a program where safety and emotional growth are at the center of the curriculum. The staff is well-trained and experienced in helping students learn to make wise choices to protect themselves and others. That commitment cannot, however, prevent students from making unwise choices.

The commitment to investigating the case was extraordinary. On the campus itself, that included the canvassing of more than 1,000 students; the formal interviewing of 150, including all students on George's floor, students residing in rooms near each trash chute on all ten floors of Wolfe Hall, and registered guests in the hall that evening; the conducting of background checks on 437 employees who could have had some knowledge of the building; the reviewing of cell phone records and the outreach to local cab companies. Once the investigation moved to the landfill, the investment of personnel continued—with almost 13,000 hours from members of the New Jersey State Police, State Police Recruits, the TCNJ Police Department, Mercer County and Bergen County Sheriff's Departments, and the Waste Management

Company. Even with this kind of support, we were not able to prevent George Smith's untimely death, nor were we able to assert with certainty the details and cause of his death.

There is no confirmation that George's death had anything to do with alcohol. There are differing descriptions of his state in the records: in the police report, witnesses reported that while he did not appear to be overly intoxicated, George had been drinking at a party off campus before he returned to Wolfe Hall, whereas the newspapers reported that some students described him as drunk. The police report indicated that he fell asleep on the floor of his friend's room on March 25. Like most other institutions of higher education with a high percentage of traditional-aged students, during my years as president, TCNJ had many cases of transports to hospitals due to alcohol abuse.

Negative results from alcohol abuse are frequent across the nation. Indeed, almost one year to the day from when George went missing, a freshman at a nearby campus fell victim to alcohol poisoning, perhaps the result of a fraternity hazing event. The statistics on alcohol poisoning for young people, particularly for freshman students, away from home for the first time, are alarming. A serious study of this issue began with the formation of a task force by the Advisory Council of the National Institute on Alcohol Abuse and Alcoholism in 1998. The goal was to provide advice to higher education leadership on intervention programs. There were 2002 and 2005 update reports. TCNJ had a program specifically focused on helping students understand the danger of alcohol abuse (Alcohol and Drug Education Program, ADEP).

In the last council report, the results were that in the eighteen-to-twenty-four age group, "alcohol-related unintentional injury deaths increased 3 percent from 1998 to 2005; binge drinking in the last month (five or more drinks in one sitting) increased from 41.7 percent to 44.7 percent, and driving while intoxicated increased from 26.5 percent to 28.9 percent" (Ralph W. Hingson, Wenxing Zha and Elisaa R. Weitzman "Magnitude of Trends in Alcohol-Related Mortality and Morbidity Among U.S. College Students Ages 18-24, 1998-2005,

Journal of Studies on Alcohol and Drugs Suppl. 2009 Jul: (16): 12-20).

This is an epidemic that permeates our culture and challenges colleges across the nation. When a student death associated with alcohol or drug abuse occurs on a campus, the statistics are powerful, but the individual loss is what really matters. The loss is inherent, and the fact that it could (or would) soon happen someplace else only makes the loss all the more painful. The tragic death of George Smith reinforces the lesson that while as campus leaders we cannot control everything, that will not stop some from seeking to blame us, nor does it minimize the responsibility we must assume in seeking to address the problem.

We must resist the temptation to confront our accusers (particularly, grieving family members), but rather seek to exert control where it might do some good. While we could never prove that George was intoxicated, the centrality of alcohol in the life of undergraduates led us to conclude that we had to continue to enhance alcohol abuse education and mental health services and support.

The spring months in 2006 were some of the hardest I had to survive as a president—not just because of the painful Smith case, but because of all the other challenges that were facing The College at the time: the historic budget cuts, the threat of intrusion of board members into the management of TCNJ in the face of these budget threats, the fallout of the proposed campus closure as one means of addressing the budget challenge, and the possible executive order that would have discouraged excellent candidates from serving on boards of trustees (see Chapter 5). In the midst of these global campus issues, the student newspaper published a cartoon with racist overtones. All required my attention. Some threatened the very future of The College—the budget, the board overreach, the possible executive order. But the horror of the Smith death took most of my emotional and professional energy during those months.

I take some pride in my being able to balance these multiple challenges: I helped the board learn to return to its lane. I was instrumental in modifying the executive order. Most importantly, I helped the campus grieve. As with every student death, no matter the circumstance, the reaction was always devastating; after each, the campus was beggared with sorrow and poor again, but after each loss, we survived, and together, we returned to some sense of normalcy.

CHAPTER 5

Props for the House

The Props assist the House
Until the House is built

—Emily Dickinson

The emotional drain of managing the Smith case was superimposed on the stress of dealing with two major actions by Governor Jon Corzine. First, there were the draconian budget cuts to higher education proposed in his draft budget, which would have cut state support for The College by over 30 percent. Second was the governor's first executive order, which would have put onerous new expectations on trustees of institutions of higher education in the state for extensive reporting and public disclosure of private holdings. I could not ignore either.

I discovered during this time the importance of identifying within a governor's office an ally with whom I could communicate my concerns about gubernatorial actions that had detrimental impact on TCNJ. In the instance of Corzine's Executive Order (EO #1), that person was the Governor's Counsel, Stuart Rabner.

Rabner knew that were the order implemented as originally written, there would have been a wholesale resignation from boards of trustees of the public institutions of higher education in New Jersey. Everyone understood the historical context for the EO: the problematic governance history of the University of Medicine and Dentistry of New Jersey (UMDNJ). In 2005, after many years of questions about management, UMDNJ agreed to a range of financial, administrative, and governance reforms, the naming of a monitor, and a Deferred Prosecution Agreement.

The US attorney who brokered this agreement was the future governor, Chris Christie. In 2006, Governor Corzine could not ignore the history, but the first version of his solution would have damaged the governance at institutions that were being governed well. Rabner worked with the presidents of the state colleges and an advisory group to help the Governor refine the order to assure that the legitimate concerns about mismanagement at institutions of higher education were addressed without discouraging citizens of the state from serving on higher education boards of trustees in the state. The Advisory Group included the President of Princeton University, two former New Jersey governors, a former attorney general of the state, and a former New Jersey supreme court justice. Representatives of the state colleges met with the group to share our concerns about the unintended consequences of the executive order as written.

On May 1, Stuart Rabner called to inform me that significant modifications were to be made to the executive order that would mitigate most of the unrealistic expectations for trustees. On May 12, Executive Order #14 was promulgated to provide the kind of guardrails to trustee actions that were viewed as necessary by political leadership, while not requiring the kind of drastic public disclosure that would have decimated the boards of trustees.

This successful resolution was the result of good work and good will on all sides. The members of the Advisory Group were individuals of exceptional stature and character. Stuart Rabner was an outstanding partner in managing the political shoals. My higher education colleagues provided reasoned and thoughtful arguments for the modification.

During this difficult time, TCNJ's trustees were anxious to prove their value to The College—particularly with regard to the budget crisis. They wanted to be seen as individuals whose expertise from the business and professional services world would be of benefit to the institution. It was also important for them to exhibit performance that distinguished theirs from the performance of trustees at UMDNJ. In this context, it was necessary to demonstrate the appearance and the fact of trustee involvement in budget preparation.

Several of my senior administrators and I engaged in extended budget planning and discussions with the leadership of the board. While this kind of intense and comprehensive discussion of budget details almost crossed the line between policy considerations (the appropriate realm of a board) and day-to-day management (the responsibility of the administration), the result of this engagement was a budget plan that was fully owned by the trustees, an extremely important outcome for that particular year. Furthermore, there was public evidence of trustee involvement. On April 18 at the first Finance and Investment Committee meeting of the TCNJ board, this budget development process began in earnest. It did not let up until the board's vote on setting tuition and fees at its July 11 meeting. The board leadership and I had to navigate this difficult path and with only a couple of missteps, I believe we did just that.

At the first meeting of the board's Finance and Investment Committee, every trustee seemed to be fully engaged with the presentation, but it was clear that some trustees had not yet appreciated the size of the extraordinary cuts that would have to be sustained by TCNJ if the governor's budget was not modified. And it was no wonder, because the recommendations were unbelievably devastating. In the third meeting of the committee, in order to bridge the revenue and expense gap, I proposed a weeklong closure of the campus to coincide with the break between semesters. This was an untested and somewhat audacious proposal, but it would result in considerable expenditure savings. There would be a week of salary savings, and utilities costs would be minimized because of the closure of all offices and most facilities for a week.

We had begun discussions with the governor's office, the Office of Employee Relations, and our local union leadership. The proposal was well-known both on and off campus, but I engaged in little or no public discussion on the campus. I was hoping that its outlandishness would capture the attention of the governor's office and reinforce the message of just how few options we had to meet the budget he was proposing. Governor Corzine was a strong union supporter, and the idea that his proposal could result in union members losing income would not be attractive to him.

Such a decision had to be the result of full-board action. In order to meet the contract with the American Federation of Teachers (AFT), unit members had to be noticed about such action at least six months before the date of the closure. Since we were planning a January closing, we would need to add a June board meeting. A week before the June 13 meeting of the board, the sunshine agenda for the board meeting was distributed. There was a frenzy of excitement and anger on the campus because the sunshine agenda included reference to a board resolution to give the president the authority to notify the members of our AFT union that, for budget reasons, we might have to close the campus for the week of January 2 through January 8, 2007.

The action would mean that all staff, including faculty and administrators, would not be paid for the period. I had quiet meetings with the presidents of all five unions on the campus and received, if not support, what seemed to be a modicum of understanding. It was particularly important to get the support of the president of the local faculty union, the AFT, Ralph Edelbach.

The night before the board meeting, the phone rang at 110 Murphy Drive, the president's house. I was not expecting a call, but I thought it was likely one of the trustees, calling with some concerns about the meeting tomorrow. It was Ralph Edelbach. He acknowledged that while he understood my rationale for the closure, he did not support it. However, he noted, none of his members either understood or supported it. He wanted me to know that there was a lot of anger and resentment on the campus. He emphasized that it would have been wiser to have shared with the full community a clear explanation of other actions taken before a closure was considered.

The next day, I published a memo with the context Ralph had suggested. Of course, the memo was too late. The faculty was enraged and those present at the Board of Trustees meeting let me know that. I was sitting at the front of Loser 116 with the chairman of the board by my side; cabinet members were sitting in the front row; there were fifty or so chairs behind the first row of chairs, and every single chair was taken. In fact, at least a dozen faculty members were standing in the back of the room.

Chair Stacy Holland opened the meeting and invited me to present my proposal for a week's closure of the campus during the winter break, a proposal made in the face of the draconian cuts to the New Jersey state colleges, particularly TCNJ, being proposed in Governor Corzine's budget. Before I could even begin my presentation, a faculty member from the Chemistry Department stood to be recognized. While it is normal protocol to register to speak at board meetings, I advised the chair that while the faculty member had not filed the required paperwork requesting to speak at a board meeting, it was best to let her speak, and that was in the authority of the chair of the board to allow.

"I cannot believe that this proposal is being taken seriously. This is contradictory to all principles of shared governance and the valuing of faculty voice."

"Believe me," I replied. "This is not an action I want to take, but I see no other option to provide a balanced budget to the board for its action in July." I explained that I would have waited until later in the year to discuss such a proposal if it were not a requirement of the AFT contract that I notify members of the unit six months before any proposed closure.

I explained to her and those present the other steps that had been taken to close the budget gap, the continuing negotiations with the legislature, the continuing campus budget reductions, and my hope that we would not have to take the closure action, but the contract required this notification if we were going to be able to use the closure as a means of effecting a balanced budget. When I emphasized that we had tried to coincide the closure with mid-winter break to cause the least disruption, she responded.

"So, you do not think that cutting someone's pay is a disruption? By the way, is everyone going to have their pay cut, including administrators?"

I confirmed that everyone, including administrators, would take the pay cut. The only difference would be that administrators would continue to work; the others (except those needed for maintaining safety on the campus) were to be furloughed. I acknowledged the negative impact of the cut in pay for everyone, particularly for members of the community like facilities staff whose salaries were at the lower end of the pay scale. Of course, no explanation was adequate to assuage the anger.

No one else spoke, but it was clear that the chemistry professor spoke for all the faculty in the room. The chair turned to the board to ask for questions. One of the trustees expressed dismay at the fact that we were having to consider such action, but no one asked any questions. I had been sharing budget modeling with the board since the original Governor's Budget Address in March so that any of their questions had already been answered.

Chair Holland then asked for a motion. Barbara Pelson made the motion to take the action; Pat Rado seconded. It passed unanimously. The faculty stood almost as one and left the room.

While in the end, I think that the proposal accomplished its purpose of being one of the messages that got through to Governor Corzine and the legislative leadership to help convince them to modify the cuts to higher education, it did a lot of damage to my support on the campus. I had not taken the time to focus on communication regarding the proposed campus closure, which resulted in unnecessary anger on the campus, particularly within the faculty union ranks.

One of the most painful examples of the loss of faculty support was from a group of faculty and staff who had joined together to recommend me for the prestigious Ralph S. Brown Award for Shared Governance. This award given by AAUP to individuals who embody the principles of shared governance is not given every year, but only when the AAUP award committee feels there is incontrovertible evidence of such commitment. I was so proud of this campus support and even more gratified to be selected. Ironically, I received the award in June 2006, only weeks after the board meeting discussing the possible campus closure. None of the recommenders for the Ralph Brown Award joined me at the award ceremony.

As further evidence of the campus resentment, when the chair of the Faculty Senate was approached by the Development Office to consider a solicitation from faculty for philanthropic support for The College, he politely declined. This refusal was pointed since in previous requests for support for the TCNJ Foundation, the Faculty Senate leadership had been generous, approaching nearly 80 percent participation rate among the senators.

Responding to the budget challenge had to be conducted in public, but some of the greatest success I had in moderating proposed political action was not conducted in a public setting. The moderation of the impact of Corzine's EO #1 is a case in point. So, also, was the pivot I used with regard to a legislative action that precluded college trustees from recommending prospective students for admission to the college for which they served as trustee (discussed in Chapter 2).

Another case in which I took the opportunity to speak out in my capacity as a college president but in a private communication was in response to President Lawrence Summers' comments at the 2005 NBER Conference on Diversifying the Science and Engineering Workforce. Summers speculated that the gender discrepancies in science, mathematics, technology, and engineering scholarship were not the result of an unequal playing field, but of a natural difference in aptitude for these types of research between men and women. Like most higher education leaders, I heard reports of these comments immediately, but I waited to speak out until I could read his words rather than depend on reportage. By February 25, the *Chronicle of Higher Education* had published Summers' remarks. By then, the Harvard faculty as well as several noteworthy higher education leaders had already published objections (including Shirley Tilghman of Princeton, Susan Hockfield of MIT, and John Hennessy of Stanford). I decided that my voice in a publication was less important than a personal letter.

I wrote President Summers a letter in which I pointed out the dismissiveness of his language and the lack of historical context of some of his comments (e.g., the failure to recognize legacy requirements, such as the importance of upper body strength to be chosen as an Air Force pilot, when currently, computers ran most of a jet's operations). I ended with a strong objection to his assertion that he was just trying to be a gadfly, not a president. As I wrote, "No college president can slough off the position at will . . . Your position as president of one of the most respected institutions in the world places the heaviest responsibility on your shoulders."

By the time my letter was received, Summers had already acted, setting up task forces to address the gender diversity issues on Harvard's campus. To his credit, however, Dr. Summers wrote me a personal response ending his letter, "I hope I have made clear that if I could turn the clock back, I would have spoken very differently."

Another example of successful behind-the-scenes communication in a political matter occurred in Chris Christie's first year as governor. While boards of trustees in the state of New Jersey are autonomous and therefore responsible specifically for setting tuition and fees for the institution they serve, it was not unusual in the final budget passed by the legislature for there to be language added to the document that in effect established a tuition budget cap—"the allocation for each institution referenced herein is predicated on the tuition increase not exceeding [x] percent, or the allocation for that institution will be reduced by twice the percentage difference above [x] percent." The legislature insisted it was not a cap, as the statute clearly empowers the individual institutional board with the establishment of institutional fees and tuition, not the legislature. But the mathematical impossibility of making up the difference between any increase above the percentage described and the reduced allocation, in effect, established a cap. While the legislature could not set tuition, it had the power to include such language in its budget proposal.

Up until Governor Christie, however, these caps were always in the discussions at the legislative level, never at the gubernatorial level. In 2010, Governor Christie included such language in his budget message. Many of my colleagues made public statements bemoaning the proposal and indicating the damage to the institutions. I instead wrote him a letter in which I explained my concerns. I had been particularly gratified by the governor's support of the expansion, rather than the diminution, of institutional autonomy at a March meeting he held with higher education leadership. While I did not include in my letter one specific fear I had about the loss of such autonomy, I did share with many others that the cap could have a negative impact on bond ratings. I did not receive a written response from Christie. A month later, the chairman of the TCNJ Board, Susanne Svizeny, sent a similar letter.

As we feared, in spring of 2010, Standard and Poor announced the downgrading of the bond ratings of New Jersey public institutions of higher education, with one of the major rationales for that downgrade being the loss of institutional autonomy in setting tuition, thereby controlling revenue. A downgrading of a bond rating results in greater costs to borrow, limiting institutional ability to garner resources for facilities upgrades, a particular problem in New Jersey, since the state had a spotty record of providing resources to state institutions for facilities. In essence, the tuition cap resulted in greater costs for institutions.

In June of 2010, Steve Adubato (a well-known New Jersey political reporter) invited two guests to one of his televised shows—Chris Christie and me. I was looking forward to the opportunity to spar with Christie. He is a great debater. While I did not always agree with him on issues of policy, I found him a smart politician, someone who was not scared of other smart people and who respected integrity.

"One of the topics I have heard a lot about in recent conversations," Adubato began, "is the proposed tuition cap for public institutions of higher education. Dr. Gitenstein, I suppose you have an opinion on that. Maybe you would want to share that with the governor?"

Before I could open my mouth, Christie responded, "Oh, let me assure you, Dr. Gitenstein has already let me know what she thinks of my proposal." He smiled, and I nodded, both knowing that we had dodged the possible embarrassing conversation that could have led to my criticizing the governor in public. I simply smiled in acknowledgement.

It is important to determine when working behind the scenes rather than making public statements is the most effective, when developing partnerships and alliances with other presidents, with other stakeholder groups, can result in better advocacy. Sometimes, however, no matter how righteous the cause, no matter how deep the commitment, such advocacy is unsuccessful.

My advocacy for a particular scholarship program consumed a lot of my attention in the early years of my presidency. New Jersey has been called the "cuckoo bird" state regarding high school graduates choosing to attend New Jersey institutions of higher education. In the early 2000s, the state was known for having the highest net outmigration of traditional-aged students in the country to attend out-of-state institutions. That is, a high percentage of New Jersey citizens sought higher education outside of the state, and few out-of-state citizens chose New Jersey for higher education. The numbers were particularly stark with the most academically talented.

In the face of these statistics, in the fiscal year of 1998, a merit-scholarship program, the Outstanding Scholar Recruitment Program (OSRP), was funded as a pilot project to reverse that trend. The structure of the program was that 50 percent of the award was to be funded by the state appropriation, and 50 percent by the individual institution. Student SAT and high school rank determined eligibility.

While students attending any public and private institution in the state could receive this support, the greatest number of OSRP students attended either Rutgers or TCNJ, because these institutions were seen as the most academically competitive of the publics in the state.

In 2004, the New Jersey Higher Education Student Assistance Authority invested in a review of the program to assess its success ("The Outstanding Scholar Recruitment Program: An Evaluation: A Report by The Institute for Higher Education Policy," Ron Phipps, Melissa Clinedinst, and Jamie Merisotis, October 2004). While the study was considered "deliberative, confidential, consultative, and advisory, and not for dissemination to the general public," the major conclusions were shared with leadership of the institutions of higher education. One of those recommendations was that OSRP should be continued and be memorialized in statute. Even in the face of this positive evaluation of OSRP and its recommendation to make the program permanent by placing it in statute, in 2006, the program was zeroed out in Governor Corzine's budget proposal.

Perhaps the program was an easy target of budget reductions, because the analysis indicated that while all institutions could benefit from the program, the real success of the program was at the public institutions, particularly at two of the twelve publics—Rutgers and TCNJ. Private institutions in New Jersey have more clout than in states with a more robust history of support for public higher education, and many of the publics felt that Rutgers and TCNJ already received an unfair portion of state dollars. If there was going to be advocacy for OSRP, it would have to be from Rutgers and TCNJ.

Support for OSRP had been cut in previous budgets, but it had never been recommended for closure. A recommendation for closure was particularly problematic because of the timing of the announcement. Many colleges, including TCNJ, offer admissions as early as the fall; part of that admission offer included a financial aid package, and part of that financial aid package would be the scholarship offer for an OSRP award. By the time Corzine announced his budget in spring of 2006, we had already made most of our offers to students who qualified for OSRP. Should Corzine's plan to eliminate the program be memorialized in the budget passed in July, TCNJ had one of two unattractive choices—either take on the state's portion of the obligation or inform students that we could not honor the full OSRP scholarship.

We had one opportunity for negotiating at least a delay in elimination. We could threaten the latter in public comments, hoping to influence legislative action. But we could not do it alone. We had to do so with our other larger, more resourced partner, Rutgers. Early conversations suggested that we would go into negotiations about retaining the program as a united front.

The competition between Rutgers and TCNJ for OSRP students was fierce. We did not attract the raw number that they did, but the percentage of OSRP students at TCNJ was much higher than at Rutgers. Rutgers likely saw an opportunity to become the institution of choice for all OSRP students. Despite the understanding that seemed to be shared in private, Rutgers began telling prospective students that they would honor the full scholarship, taking on the state's burden.

Clearly, TCNJ had to take the same action. The impact of the closure of OSRP ended up being most destructive to TCNJ because of our success in attracting these students. According to the study of OSRP, in 2003 to 2004, 431 of the 1,441 students who met the OSRP standards statewide matriculated at TCNJ, which resulted in 39 percent of the entering class at TCNJ being OSRP-eligible, the highest in the state. TCNJ agreed to honor what would have been the state obligation for the cohort of students who entered as freshmen in fall of 2006, pending their maintaining academic eligibility, for their four years at The College. But it would be prohibitive to extend such a costly scholarship program to future cohorts. In other words, the last year of OSRP at TCNJ was for the cohort of students who entered in 2006.

The decision to cut the funding for OSRP was a great failure of vision by the state, which had tremendous negative impact on The College, both in terms of admissions and finances (as we substituted some institutional dollars for what should have been state dollars for the cohort of students who had been promised OSRP in their financial aid package). To this day, I wonder what other strategies could have been used to preserve the program. It was one of the times when I learned that collaborations with other institutions can be tenuous, and we cannot assume that our sense of shared interest will be the same as our putative partner. This was a case when it was each institution for itself.

The single most dangerous political fight which I had to wage behind the scenes involved a problematic building project. In 2002 to 2003, we concluded that TCNJ needed to add to and upgrade our on-campus housing opportunities. The facilities would need to be attractive for upper-class students. They would have to be apartment-style living rather than old-fashioned residence hall living. Our plan was to work with a contractor to use modular units, hoping to facilitate the speed to completion.

Early in April 2004, I asked Vice President Pete Mills if I could take a tour of the construction. When I walked up to the second floor of the building, I was shocked to see the disarray of the site. The units and the construction itself were filled with mold, and there seemed to be little order to the workplace. I'd never seen so much mold. I'd never seen red as well as black mold. I was appalled not only at the state of the project, but also that I had not been informed of any of the problems; this situation did not happen overnight.

The fallout was expansive. Students had been banking on the new living situation for the fall of 2004. We had to change the entire process whereby students were assigned housing on the campus, throwing the housing program into disarray. The lottery for housing that year had to allow students who had expected these new accommodations to have preference for on-campus living, but it would be in the less attractive, older facilities. Furthermore, we felt that we needed to provide not only financial compensation, but also guaranteed housing for the next year as well, should the second building not be completed.

Over the next ten months, The College tried to negotiate a deal with the construction company. The offers from the construction company were completely unacceptable, as they not only required continued investment of institutional dollars, but they also offered no real deadline for completion. In the end, we had to reach out to the surety company and the insurance commissioner and finally take action to throw the construction company off the site.

While on the face of it, our plan of action seemed obvious, there were two important factors that made some of the trustees more willing to continue negotiating. First, we really did need these housing options for our students. Second, this particular construction company had close ties to a powerful state senator.

One trustee who was well-known in both political and real estate circles in New Jersey urged me to keep negotiating with the construction company, to work out a business deal, to be sensitive to the fact that the company had powerful friends in the state senate. I objected. This was not my money; it was not even The College's money; it was the students' money. Fortunately, on this matter, the trustees as a whole agreed with my position.

One of the reasons that the Metzger Drive Apartments project became such a problem was because I was not informed when the difficulties first arose on the project. There are many presidents and CEOs who communicate to their staff that if the news is bad, fix it and don't let them know. I am just the opposite. The worst thing a subordinate could do was find out about some problem and not alert me to the facts. I observed early on in my leadership journey the negative consequences of the senior leadership being kept in the dark, both in higher education and in the larger business community.

In 2002, when Sarbanes-Oxley was passed, I was a director of a mutual fund board. I came home from a board meeting and turned to my cabinet and said that I knew Sarbanes-Oxley had nothing to do with the nonprofit sector, but I was confident that this kind of oversight was coming our way. We needed to start thinking about how we set up structures that assure transparency and disclosure regarding auditing procedures at TCNJ. In 2004 to 2005, the Board of Trustees conducted a thorough review of the bylaws of the board, and by February 2005, a newly constituted Audit, Risk Management, and Compliance Committee became a strong partner with the administration in facilitating the goals of transparency and disclosure.

In support of this new focus, in 2007, I searched for and hired the first General Counsel for The College, and Thomas Mahoney began to build a robust office that included support for the board committee, an enhanced internal audit function, an Office of Compliance, and a thoroughly developed Enterprise Risk Management process. This was accomplished at least two years before most of my colleagues focused attention on such matters.

My attention to these additional functions was based on my strong belief that the most important feature of a healthy organization is knowing and facing the facts, whether they be good or bad. When I look at many of the recent scandals on college and university campuses (Penn State, Michigan State, University of North Carolina at Chapel Hill), one of the underlying causes is the failure of the CEO to be aware of systemic problems. That failure is sometimes the result of complex and siloed organizations, but sometimes that failure is the result of a CEO communicating to subordinates that their job is to fix a problem and to give the CEO plausible deniability in the face of legal and ethical institutional lapses. That was not my message, and everyone knew it.

As early as 2010, I learned that the community understood my expectations. The higher education media was filled with the sordid details of the academic integrity problems in the athletic department at Chapel Hill. I was walking down the hall of the second floor of Green Hall (the main administrative building) and saw two colleagues chatting. I could not hear what they were saying, but I could tell they were laughing. Stacy Schuster, Executive Director of College Relations, and Matt Golden, Executive Director of Public Affairs and Strategic Programs, were administrative stars, early in their careers.

When I asked them what was so funny, they responded that they were talking about the morass at Chapel Hill. They couldn't understand the culture there, but they were sure they knew what would happen if anyone at TCNJ tried to hide a similar potential scandal. That person would be fired.

The support of colleagues during the times of political difficulty and campus crisis is essential. That support for me was sometimes simply a phone message, sometimes it was a public statement. My closest colleague in the New Jersey public higher education sector was George Pruitt, President of Thomas Edison State University (TESU). In many ways, our institutions could not have been more different, but in many ways, our approach to leadership was totally in sync. TESU was an institution focusing on the needs of adult students, using portfolio and distance education long before it became integrated into many institutions' strategies, and providing a wide range of graduate as well as undergraduate programing. TCNJ focused on the needs of traditional-aged students in a residential setting, providing some graduate, but mostly undergraduate programming. What the two institutions had in common was that during our tenures as presidents, George and I both recognized the importance of the distinctiveness of missions, and that while we did not compete for students, together we served the citizens of the state of New Jersey and the region with quality alternatives for higher education. Most importantly, both of us were totally committed to the principles of fair play and equity in education and in interpersonal interaction.

We both could depend on one another in specific situations, and sometimes, in general, everyday frustrations. Once when I was dealing with a negative State Comptroller's report regarding mandatory fees at several state institutions, including The College, I simply had to blow off steam, so I called George.

The audit had found fault in institutional transparency about the use of the fees at several New Jersey institutions. Particularly with regard to TCNJ, they took exception to the fact that in our budget plans, we raised fees for tuition and mandatory fees at the same percentage, rather than distinguishing methodologies between the two revenue sources. They maintained that we did not rigorously separate funds for each fee. I put in a call to George's office. He called back two hours later.

Without any introduction, I simply began cursing. "Those a-holes. Do they have any idea what it is to run an institution of higher education in New Jersey? Have they even looked at our Tuition Hearing materials where we describe exactly how the increases in fees and tuition are used? Have they asked the students or the families? Idiots and f-ing a-holes."

George just listened and then said, "Well, do you feel better?" In fact, I did.

The props that supported me were not only individuals, but values (student-centeredness, attention to mission, ethics) so that even in those most threatening of times. I could affirm the soul not just of myself, but of the institution.

CHAPTER 6

The Pod of Revolution

*Revolution is the Pod
Systems rattle from*
—**Emily Dickinson**

Developing a leadership team is one of the most important jobs of a new president. Cultivating a leadership team by responding to changes in the environment and in the members of the team is one of the most important jobs of a president throughout his or her tenure. Running an organization as complex as an institution of higher education requires expertise in all areas of the enterprise—academic affairs, finance, human resources, information resources, legal affairs, facilities management, student affairs, government and community relations, and fundraising. No one person is an expert in every single one, but a president must be able to understand the challenges of each and select senior executives with special expertise in each of these areas. The president must be self-confident enough to select people who are better in a specific discipline than she but also individuals who are able to work together in a team and provide insights and advice to the president.

While this job of building a strong leadership team is always an important challenge for an incoming president, it was particularly acute at TCNJ when I became president because of the important differences between me and my predecessor. Harold Eickhoff was a successful president, leading The College for almost twenty years, building on the vision and insights of his predecessor, Clayt Brower.

Dr. Eickhoff was instrumental in working with colleagues and Governor Thomas Kean in transforming public higher education in the state of New Jersey. Governor Kean and President Eickhoff embraced the importance of institutional distinctiveness, placing TCNJ as a competitive public alternative to private higher education, focusing on traditional-aged students, the importance of residential education, and commitment to high-quality academic programs and facilities. This part of Harold's vision attracted me to the position in the first place. There should be a place in the public sector where lower- and middle-class students can be challenged and educated without paying the private school tuition and fees. There were, however, important differences between Harold's and my vision for the future of TCNJ, as well as important differences between us as leaders.

First, I centered my identity as a leader in my identity as an academic with my focus on academic programs; Harold focused his energies on student development through the student affairs programs, including athletics. When I had visited the campus for the onsite interview in 1998, I was struck by the shelves in the president's office—filled with awards and photographs, but no books. I knew that my version of the president's office would be quite different—not only would it be filled with books, but with books that made a statement about who I was. Second, Harold had an authoritarian leadership style. I have always been committed to a concept of team leadership. It was not that I did not have strong opinions about the direction of The College, it was that I believed the success of The College would be greater if my opinions were informed by the input of multiple talented professionals.

In addition, Harold's definition of institutional success focused much more on externals and inputs (the look of the campus and student SATs and high school rank) rather than my interest in academic program transformation to meet the current needs of students, society, and outputs (the graduation rate of students, along with their placement in graduate programs, in high paying and satisfying jobs, or both). My greater interest in program and outputs benefited tremendously from my ability to build a real leadership team, as did my deep appreciation for the importance of shared governance and working closely with the faculty and academic leadership to update the curriculum.

Other than the president, the most important member of the cabinet is the Vice President of Academic Affairs and Provost. When I joined TCNJ, there was not a strong tradition for this kind of position. Indeed, the center of gravity on the cabinet was not a presidential partnership with Academic Affairs, but with the Vice President of Finance and Administration. This change in title and appreciation of the centrality of the provost would be absolutely essential in accomplishing my vision to transform the curriculum. Having seen the importance of a real provost at Drake, I wanted to establish a similar model for TCNJ.

Almost as soon as I joined in January 1999, I began the national search for that position. Our first attempt to appoint by the end of that first spring semester was not successful, but by the fall, we had identified several talented finalists, and by October 1999, I had appointed Stephen Briggs, Dean of the Faculty at Rollins College. Steve had all the requisite experience and qualifications. He was a true academic; he provided a different intellectual perspective to my humanities training; he had intellectual taste. Steve proved to be instrumental in fleshing out exactly what a real provost is, how important the role is to the academic integrity of an institution, reinforcing how the partnership with the president is foundational to the success of any institution of higher education. He led the curricular transformation that was one of the most important accomplishments of my tenure. He took on difficult faculty and student disciplinary issues.

Perhaps the most important success in the early years of my presidency was the Academic Transformation. Steve and I shared a vision of a review of the curriculum that would not only update the undergraduate curriculum to meet new expectations in society for students with hands-on experience and sophisticated critical thinking skills, but it would also allow students and faculty to work more closely on research projects.

A simplistic way of describing the change was that the full curriculum needed to be changed from a basic three-hour credit format to a basic four-hour credit format. Steve rightly insisted, however, that this simplistic description of the transformation did not capture the change in curriculum that nurtured both a more intense relationship between students and faculty and a space for faculty scholarship. Such a change required revision of every single course, every single major, every single minor, every single concentration.

The faculty's first response to this challenge was shock, and in some cases, resistance. Some faculty worried about how they would repackage introductory courses to meet accreditation, how they would assure that students received the same information necessary to flourish after graduation. The more structured the discipline (such as physics,) the more animated the objections. I responded that I was sure that there were other institutions that had four-credit-hour structures that met accreditation and disciplinary standards, and that our faculty was just as talented and creative as faculty at these sister institutions.

After many town halls led by the provost, I could tell that we had won over a critical mass of the faculty. They could see the value of this greater opportunity to work with our exceptional students. They could see the added value of additional time for their own research. Student-faculty research and greater engagement of students with faculty mentors outside the class hour represented that extra hour per class.

At the last town hall, I told the faculty that I was confident that the transformation would reinforce TCNJ's distinctiveness as a public institution, offering the kind of quality education that people expect at the more elite privates. I believed that in years to come, we would be able to prove that success by the number of our students who entered the academy and the acceptance rate of our students in competitive graduate programs. By the same token, I made sure that the faculty understood that there had to be a definite end date for discussion. I clearly wanted the faculty to lead this discussion and frame the program, but there had to be a time limit here.

"I will give you two years to complete the framework. If you do not, I am sure that Steve and I will be able to create it ourselves." I smiled and—let's say—most of the faculty laughed.

And that's indeed what happened. Within three years, every program (even in the Physics Department) had revised all their courses and programs. Within ten years, the National Science Foundation ranked TCNJ as second (behind Princeton) in New Jersey for baccalaureate-origin institutions of PhD recipients. In 2016, the Council on Undergraduate Research (CUR) recognized TCNJ as an exemplar in student-engaged learning.

Six years later, Steve wrote, "Thank you for letting me be your provost. I'm proud of what we've accomplished together, especially the kind of culture we've nurtured, and I'll long be in your debt."

After Steve left to become President of Berry College, I found it difficult to identify a person with the same commitment to this vision of a real "second" at The College. In 2013, when I appointed Jacqueline Taylor, founding Dean of the College of Communication at DePaul University in Chicago, I felt that I had identified just such a "second." Our partnership was a productive one, resulting in a forward-thinking strategic plan that provided the foundation for my final years at TCNJ. On the one-year anniversary of her appointment, she returned from a trip to California to a box of chocolates from me. She wrote, "Today is my one-year anniversary. You are the best boss I have ever had. I am thrilled to be your provost." It is no wonder that I gave her a copy of the document that Mick shared with me, tongue-in-cheek, but with some recognition of the javelin-catching aspects of the provost job. The source was the 1629 Articles of War, issued by Charles I:

The Provost must have a horse allowed him and some soldiers to attend him and all the rest commanded to obey and assist or else the service will suffer; for he is but one man and must correct many and therefore he cannot be beloved. And he must be riding from one Garrison to another to see the soldiers do not outrage nor scath the country.

Building a team is not always created through addition of talented colleagues. It is sometimes the result of helping a member of the leadership team transition out of a position. In a couple of cases, the need for the transition was because the incumbent created a toxic work environment in their unit. While in my experience, the problem was always a single individual, the problem affected the entire unit, and the toxicity of problematic leadership in one unit can bleed out into the entire organization. In these cases, it was necessary to conduct an objective third party review, not merely depend on the criticisms that just happened to make it to the president's office. Furthermore, unless there was evidence of real malfeasance, the goal was to create a respectful exit for the individual, either to another opportunity within the organization, or to retirement. Often, these opportunities were seen for how they were intended—as platforms for a position outside The College. But there is no value in humiliating a former colleague. The goal is to remove a problematic individual from leadership and thereby improve the leadership team.

There were at least two times when retirement allowed me to make significant changes not only in the culture of the senior leadership team, but also in the structure of the cabinet. When I joined TCNJ, I did not begin by asking former cabinet members to submit resignations and start with a clean slate. I know of presidents who do that, but such actions can have unintended consequences, including the loss of institutional memory. There were, however, some changes that eventually needed to be made because of the significant difference in philosophy of leadership between me and my predecessor.

The most significant such change entailed a revisioning of a position that consolidated too much responsibility in one division and by so doing undermined the concept I was trying to promote that the second officer of The College was the Provost and Vice President of Academic Affairs. This was a difficult and delicate process, because the person in this job was good at his job; his span of control was just too large. When I arrived at TCNJ, the Vice President for Administration and Finance was responsible for budget and finance (which included financial aid), facilities management (which included both maintenance and construction), real estate, police services, student services, and human resources. Clearly, that array and depth of responsibilities made him the second officer of TCNJ.

It took me several years, but I eventually redesigned the cabinet such that responsibilities were more broadly distributed. There was a Vice President for Administration who was responsible for facilities, construction, real estate, and police; a Vice President for Human Resources; a Vice President for Student Services and Information Technology; and a Vice President for Enrollment Management. This redefinition of roles provided more informed and diverse input into cabinet and presidential decisions and by default elevated the provost's role. Harold's Vice President for Administration and Finance maintained a strong commitment to the institution for the five years that we worked together, but he never felt comfortable with either my approach to leadership or with the change in responsibilities for his role. In 2004, he retired after thirty-three years at The College.

In addition to building a team intentionally, there are times when a leader is known by how she handles a difficult administrative change that brings with it negative press. During my time at TCNJ, the saddest such occasion was in the follow-up to a resignation of a much beloved senior administrator. Al Bridges was well known throughout higher education in New Jersey. He was chosen as the person to host Don during our on-campus interview, to help introduce us to the social aspects of living in Central Jersey. While serving as Vice President of Government and Community Affairs during my early years as president, Al also was elected mayor of Ewing, the town in which TCNJ was situated.

In March 2002, Al joined me for his regularly scheduled one-on-one. We had completed the planned agenda, and Al surprised me with his announcement that he intended to resign from his position. He shared no details, but he was adamant. Four months later, an article was published in the *Trentonian*, a local newspaper, that put Al's resignation in context. My heart was broken by what was revealed, and I felt intense anger at those who sought to trade on the salaciousness of the story—the trustee who was dying to tell me more gossip, the staff who loved to see a senior executive fall.

The article, apparently based on divorce documents, included details of a life 180 degrees antithetical to the Al many of us thought we knew. There were tales of drug use, infidelity, failure to make utility payments, and even violent treatment of his wife. Several months later, the *Trenton Times* reported that Al had pleaded guilty to possession of crack cocaine. When the *Signal*, the student newspaper, reached out to me for a comment, I replied, "It's very sad. He had a long, great career. I was shocked when I heard the news."

Within days, The College was contacted by the external press for a statement. I knew it was coming, but I was still surprised, and I made clear how it should be handled. No matter what the article included, I knew a completely different person. I was not going to depend on anyone in the public relations office to draft the response. I dictated what was going to be the institutional statement.

"Al Bridges has been a devoted colleague and friend to members of the TCNJ community for decades. Our thoughts and prayers are with him and his family during these difficult times."

During a leadership team meeting the next week, a director asked what we should say when asked about Al, and I responded that they had The College statement. That was what was to be said. Period. Full stop.

Leadership at an institution of higher education must also consider the complex governance structure that is typical of a healthy academic organization. Leadership must incorporate not just the administration and staff roles, but also the faculty's role in shared governance and the authority of the trustees as fiduciaries of the institution. At TCNJ and all public institutions in New Jersey (and some private ones), shared governance was made especially complex because the faculty was also unionized. I have always believed in the importance of faculty voice in the leadership of colleges and universities. I believe that better decisions are made when appropriate consultation has involved all stakeholders before a major decision.

Indeed, in my tenure as president, several times when I was less successful were times when I made a misstep in such consultation. I do believe, however, that there are two important features that need to be added to this discussion on shared governance. First, I do not believe that only faculty should have a voice in the future of the institution. Staff and students should as well. This complicates the project, but as with good, shared governance with faculty, the result is a better outcome. Second, consultation does not require that there be unanimity of opinion before action. If that were the case, no controversial decision could be made, no transformative action could be taken.

There must be documents to clarify shared understandings about the responsibility and the locus of input for each stakeholder group. The more difficult the problem, the less likely there will be unanimity. While not welcomed by all stakeholders in all cases, the governance structure requires that it is the administration that must take actionable recommendations to the board, and it is the board that has the responsibility for acting on those recommendations.

In addition, there is an inherent contradiction in the perspective of a union and that which is embedded in the principles of shared governance. A union represents the singular perspective of a unit, usually in conflict with management, administration, or both. In shared governance, each contributing member works with representatives of other stakeholder groups to help craft a collective recommendation to the administration. The administration takes this recommendation under advisement and then crafts a recommendation that is taken by the president to the board. This is a tightrope that every president of a college with unionized employees must walk. The faculty as governance partners works with the administration in the development of curriculum and program, but as union members, the relationship is management and employee, not the context for strategic planning or visioning.

An essential partner in leading a college is the Board of Trustees. The relationship between senior administration and the governing board can be tricky, and particularly so in the public sector, because of how trustees become members and because of the relatively short tenure of public institution trustees. At TCNJ, like the other four-year regional institutions in New Jersey, trustees were recommended by the governor and confirmed by the state senate.

By its very nature, the process was political. While there was the opportunity for the president through the Board of Trustees to recommend prospective trustees, there was no guarantee that the rationale for someone's being appointed because of a particular expertise or alumni status would have an impact on the calculations of the governor's Appointment Secretary. Sometimes, we were fortunate in getting our recommendations taken seriously, and sometimes, even when we received unknown or unaffiliated members as trustees, the service of the trustee was exemplary.

My favorite example of such a circumstance was early in my tenure, in 1999, when we were informed that Governor Whitman would be recommending a billboard CEO for membership on the TCNJ board. The board chair and I asked for the opportunity to meet with the candidate to get to know him and to share expectations for service on the board.

When Heather Fehn, assistant to the board, told Chairman Gladstone and me that Mr. McAndrews, the trustee candidate, had arrived, she had a skeptical look on her face. The door opened, and Jimmy McAndrew entered. He had a broad smile and was dressed in a long brown leather coat. Underneath a large black cowboy hat, he sported a long ponytail.

I could tell that Bob was as dubious as I was. Clearly, Heather had her own reservations. Then we began to talk. Jimmy had done his homework. When asked about why he wanted to be a trustee at TCNJ, he said that he knew that TCNJ had come to be seen as the academic gem of the state colleges. It was known as a public ivy, which he knew brought with it some resentment and suspicion from some sectors, but surely a state like New Jersey should have such an institution, one that could serve to keep the best and the brightest in the state for their college years, and perhaps for their years of work. He spoke with conviction. By the end of our hour-long conversation, Bob and I were questioning our initial read. Later, I learned that Jimmy had greeted Heather as "sweetheart," which explained her skeptical look when she introduced him to Bob and me.

When Jimmy stepped down from the board in 2010, I recognized that he was one of the most thoughtful, engaged, supportive, and creative trustees I ever knew. During the difficult conversations regarding the mold-filled Metzger Drive Apartment project, Jimmy was one of the most supportive and articulate trustees on taking the difficult but correct stance with the construction company. He understood the possible negative repercussions of my plan of action but agreed that my recommendation was based on sound principle and rationale and was the best strategy.

He was also a strong supporter of one of our most innovative and socially conscious programs. Professor Michelle Tartar integrated her students' writing on social justice with multiple trips to a nearby women's prison, where the students helped the inmates improve their writing skills and the inmates broadened the experience of the students in understanding the impact of incarceration. Jimmy's financial support helped fund one of the imaginative student engagement projects first envisioned by the Academic Transformation.

Not all candidates who came to trusteeship at TCNJ were so productive. Two candidates whose names came directly from the governor's office whose backgrounds and credentials, unlike Jimmy's, suggested that they would have been perfect additions to the board turned out to be ineffective trustees. One was a recent graduate with close ties to the union movement in New Jersey. The other had a spectacular academic pedigree, complete with a doctorate from an Ivy League school.

Their attendance at meetings was spotty at best. One dedicated trustee wrote an email to one absentee colleague (who was officially a trustee for seven years but was present at only a couple of meetings) indicating that he hoped the colleague would actually show up at the next board meeting so that the experienced trustee could meet his new colleague. Despite his perennial absence, this individual had a hobby horse about his very own concept of governance that disrupted board deliberations on the few occasions when he did attend a meeting.

However individuals became trustees at TCNJ, I sought to nurture them as full partners, creating opportunities for substantive leadership of the institution while helping guide that leadership to remain at the strategic and generative level (asking questions and guiding the direction without attempting to manage the day-to-day operations). During my presidency, TCNJ created new committees that required special expertise. First, we created the Audit, Compliance, and Risk Management Committee, depending on individuals with informed knowledge of finance and risk management. Second, we institutionalized a Governance Committee that guided the board in self-assessment and enhancement of board education. These committees and the encouragement of strong individuals to engage actively but appropriately with the governance of The College required courage and patience on my part. During my tenure as president, this change in direction devolved entirely to the benefit of TCNJ.

The most important member of the board for a successful leadership team with the president is the chair. During my time at TCNJ, there were seven different chairs. Well over half were excellent—each in different ways, but each adding important value to the board's deliberations and the future health of The College. The problematic leaders were those who confused the responsibility of the board with that of the management of the college and those who, as I liked to say, "knew the price of everything and the value of nothing."

What the good chairs could do was partner with me as president in guiding the board in deliberations, from something as complex as how to manage sexual assault on campus to issues like how to set the tuition and fees. With the support, guidance, and input of excellent board chairs, TCNJ was successful in implementing the transformed curriculum, finalizing a complex public-private partnership that added residential and retail opportunities for students and the township, managing crises of student deaths, managing the steadily dropping financial support from the state, and fending off the attempts by political forces to intrude in the governance and mission of The College.

The promise of the institution was the pod of revolution that shook the stalks of the past to assure that creativity and future thinking was not dead.

CHAPTER 7

Selecting Your Own Society

The Soul selects her own Society—
Then—shuts the Door—

—Emily Dickinson

Don's sixtieth birthday was September 19, 2001. We had a wonderful weekend planned, beginning on September 15, 2001. We had invited family and friends from across the country as well as new contacts from New Jersey. Our children, Pauline and Sam, would be home from college, Pauline from Earlham College and Sam from Carnegie-Mellon University. It was going to be a fabulous celebration.

Then, those planes flew into the World Trade Center and the Pentagon and crashed into the field in Shanksville, Pennsylvania. The world stopped. No planes were flying anywhere in the United States. No one was in the mood for celebration. As much as I loved Don, I had to turn my entire focus to the mental health of the students, faculty, and staff on the TCNJ campus.

Six months later, we had a sixty-and-a-half birthday celebration on March 23, 2002. It was a wonderful event, though threaded through the evening was the realization of why we had had to reschedule. The comments by friends and family really captured the amazing intellect and humor that is Donald Hart.

JoAnn Williams, who we have known for over half a century and has been at every major family event in our lives, wrote a poem:

Oh, listen my children and ye shall hear
Of the ancient philosopher sitting here
This bearded one in his sixtieth year
A wise old man, almost a seer

. . . I was told this occasion is really a roast . . .

After thirty-four years I can say, alas,
Can be a real **"Pain in the ass"**

Don's older brother, Tom, who knew Don the longest, wrote that what captured Don's real essence was his intelligence. He believed that Don's brain just grew more quickly than the rest of his body, and that made him a terror in many high school classes, as he enjoyed correcting teachers who mispronounced words while pouring over his recently acquired dictionary. Tom remembered how teachers complained that Don read "too many damned books." Tom concluded that while by birth he was elder, he came to look up to Don as if he were the older brother, describing him as "the most intelligent and inquisitive human being I'd ever really been allowed to get to know so well and over such an extended period of time."

David Williamson, a friend from our hometown of Florala, Alabama, reminisced about the Hart brothers' positions as drum major in the high school band. He offered as evidence of Don's ability to learn that when Tom was drum major, the band marched behind the horses in parade, but when Don was drum major, they marched in front of the horses. Mark, my brother, remembered a fantastic adventure in

New York City when Don planned a trip for Mark, my sister-in-law, Libby, me, and Don to Queens to try out a new Indian restaurant that had been reviewed in the *New York Times*. The adventure included an hour-long bus ride to Queens, "so we could see the city," a delicious meal at a hole in the wall which took us forty minutes to find by foot, and a blessedly shorter ride back to Manhattan on the subway.

In my remarks, I remembered the wide range of topics Don had taught me: Navy words for certain body parts, the structure of the sonata allegro, and why a Komodo dragon bite is so poisonous. I remarked on his amazing dedication to me and our children and the fact that he had followed me into a lot of different situations, including a culvert during a flash flood.

I ended:

> let's face it, he's got the best beard in the room. And those blue eyes, they can warm your soul, or, I have heard from others who have received "the look," they can freeze your blood.
> But for me, Don, [and I quoted e. e. cummings]
> > somewhere I have never traveled, gladly beyond
> > any experience, your eyes have their silence

It was a tremendous joy to host a seventy-fifth party for Don fifteen years later, one that did not have the overlay of sorrow of the one in 2002. Many of the same friends and family were in attendance, but also many new friends. I could see that the love and admiration from the older acquaintances were now echoed by all the people we had gotten to know and love during the TCNJ years. The invitation read: "Age is just a (BIG) number, and this year Donald B. Hart's Number is VERY BIG."

While the experiences that involved Don were sometimes challenging, the ones with our children, Sam and Pauline, brought even greater complexities. It is one thing to expect your spouse or life partner to participate in the difficulties and exposure that comes with belonging to a presidential family. In many ways, the partner goes into the situation with eyes open. It's quite another to have such expectations for a child. They have little choice in the matter.

One of the most painful examples in my life of this impact on presidential families was the impact that my accepting the job at TCNJ had on my son, Sam. The year I was appointed president, Pauline was already attending Earlham College, but Sam was a junior in high school. My tenure at TCNJ was to begin mid-year. We were confronted with a difficult decision. Did I defer considering all administrative opportunities outside Des Moines, Iowa, until his graduation, remaining in an almost untenable situation at Drake University? Did I accept the position at The College of New Jersey and figure out a way for Sam to remain in Des Moines to finish his junior year or even finish high school?

While the latter was attractive, Don and I were not willing to live apart for one-and-a-half years. We had done that for a year while I worked at SUNY central. We were all miserable. We did not know another family well enough to consider asking them to host Sam in West Des Moines for that period. We made the hard decision for me to accept the job at TCNJ and for Sam to transfer to Hopewell Valley High School in Pennington, New Jersey, where the president's house was sited. While Pennington was primarily an upper-middle-class White community, it was more diverse than West Des Moines (where I liked to say dark hair signified diversity), and Hopewell Valley was quite good. But the fact of the matter is that moving a high school junior to a new environment, a new school, particularly in the middle of a school year, is a cruel choice.

I do not know if that was the right decision, but I do know that Sam was appropriately angry about the move and his lack of agency in the choice. It was unfair, but at the time, Don and I thought it was the best decision for the family. If I could go back, perhaps I would make a different choice, because I regret the pain it caused my son. But that choice would not have been to leave Sam in Des Moines. It would have been to not accept the job at TCNJ.

The fact that she was the daughter of the president of a college also had an impact on our daughter's life. Pauline, like Sam, was never anonymous, and so many of the decisions we had to make in any celebration or event had to consider my position. For instance, when she decided to marry, we determined that we would hold the ceremony on the campus in the Spiritual Center and the celebration after the ceremony at the president's house. I was careful in the arrangements that everything we did would be above reproach, that there would be not just no impropriety, but no appearance of impropriety. Thus, we carefully documented paying for everything. We paid the catering service the going rate for their services. We paid the going rate for the facilities we rented on campus, and we proposed paying a fee for the use of our own house during the hours of the wedding dinner dance.

Pauline was without a doubt the most wonderful bride—sharing every minute planning the event with her husband-to-be, Ellis Barber, and his mother, Sandra Barber. They were thrilled to be part of the planning and enjoyed shaping a special event for the young couple. The only time I saw a glimpse of a Bridezilla was one day when Pauline came over to the house for a meeting. It was perhaps five days before the May 22, 2010 wedding.

"Mom, what is that in the backyard? What is *that* in the . . ."

I looked out, and there was a backhoe right on the edges of the beautiful, wooded area that I knew was doomed to provide a larger lot for the new McMansion planned for the property behind us. I had been told that the construction was not to begin until June, but there, in plain sight, a backhoe.

Pauline was almost hyperventilating, thinking that the backdrop for her lovely, tented dinner dance was going to be a large piece of construction equipment. I assured her that I would get the new neighbors to move the backhoe, or I would learn how to drive it myself. Two days later, the backhoe was out of sight. It did not appear for another two weeks, so Pauline and Ellis' dinner tent was decorated only with festive lanterns and not lights from a backhoe.

Most special for me was to watch how others from the TCNJ community, people who worked in the catering arm of Sodexo, The College's partner in food services, as well as The College staff in Conference and Event Services (CES) got to see what a special person Pauline is and come to enjoy the planning almost as much as the family. It was one of those celebrations that captured a person's generosity and openness, but there was an awareness that the planning, the removal of surprising backhoes, and the celebration itself—all were under a spotlight.

Only two years later, on May 4, 2012, Pauline again had to experience one of life's most seminal moments under the harsh light of my position coloring the event. This time, it was a horrible, sudden death.

Don was in Manhattan at our apartment on 56th street; I was attending a meeting of the Middle States Association in Philadelphia. Pauline called me at 5 a.m. Ellis had collapsed and the EMTs were in their apartment.

"Can you come?"

She was crying; I could hear it in her voice, but she seemed in control.

They were taking him to Robert Wood Johnson Hamilton. I told Pauline we would meet her there.

I called Don, and we developed a plan. He took New Jersey Transit (NJT) from Penn Station to Hamilton, New Jersey. I took Southeastern Pennsylvania Transportation Authority (SEPTA) from Philadelphia to Trenton and NJT to Hamilton. By the time we got to the hospital, a large contingent of Barber family members were there. Ellis' parents and his paternal grandmother looked up as we entered and greeted us with warmth and a deep sadness. The news was not good. Pauline was holding up well until the very end when it became clear that the internal bleeding was too extensive for Ellis to be saved.

Pauline began to wail; Ellis's grandmother sat quietly, inconsolable in a chair by herself; Sandra, Ellis' mother, was surrounded by her husband and Jermaine, her other son. I went to Pauline to try to console her. She pushed me away. I never felt so helpless in my life.

It was not an experience I ever could have imagined. Of course, my loss was nothing like that being experienced by the Barbers, but seeing my daughter lose her dream of a long life with someone she loved was painful beyond words. Pauline's loss was devastating.

On the second day after Ellis' death, Pauline was sitting on the couch in their apartment on Mary Street in Bordentown, playing with her cats when she said, "You know, people say the stupidest things when someone dies. I mean what does it mean: 'This is God's plan.' What plan? What about *my* plan?"

At Ellis' funeral, the room was filled with Barber family members and many of Ellis' friends. Sam and his girlfriend (who later became his wife) Karen flew in from San Francisco. Two of my nieces (Sarah Gitenstein from Chicago and Hannah Assadi from Brooklyn) joined us. And there in the back was almost every member of the senior executive leadership team of TCNJ, a large contingent from the police department, and two trustees. I was deeply moved, and Don could tell I was about to break down. He knew I would never want that to happen in this situation.

"Hey, Bobby, who do you think is running the place?"

It gave me a moment to smile. Then the ceremony started. I doubt that Pauline was even aware of the people from TCNJ, but I was, and their support meant the world to me and helped me make it through the funeral. Pauline was a heroine; she had insisted that she speak. She stood in the front of all those people, with her brother by her side, and she talked about Ellis. Sam was so loving and supportive; the whole scenario brought me to tears—tears of sorrow and pride. I have never been prouder of my daughter, and until my son married and became the amazing father that he is, I'd never been prouder of him. Sam said nothing in words but stood holding his sister's hand.

The impact of the personal on the role as president is not always ceremonial or dramatic, but it can be meaningful. In the 2016 to 2017 academic year, I began conversations with Chairman Caballero about my intent to retire. It just seemed like the right time. We had finished a successful first capital campaign; I had been at the college for almost eighteen years; TCNJ was in good shape financially and reputationally; I was approaching seventy; announcing in the summer of 2017 would give The College a year to conduct a thorough national search for my successor to be appointed by the summer of 2018.

In the spring of 2018, as my July 1 retirement date approached, I knew that I had to begin cleaning out my office. My office was filled with my most prized collection of books, a rather substantial Judaica collection, novels by authors ranging from Saul Bellow to Cynthia Ozick to Abraham Cahan, literary criticism running the gamut, and my most prized books: 172 books on and in Yiddish. Many of the English volumes of my Judaica collection could be gifted to the TCNJ Library (fifty-two new titles, comprising some sixty-two volumes and at least double that amount that were duplicates of what the library already owned), but the Yiddish books needed to find another home. No one using the TCNJ Library was likely to need a Yiddish text. I reached out to the Yiddish Book Center in Amherst, Massachusetts, and found a welcoming response.

In the afternoon of March 29, I got a call from Zeke Levine. We had an appointment for him to come to my office the next day to look at my collection of Yiddish titles. Unfortunately, the van that they were supposed to use had just had some mechanical troubles. He wondered if we could find another time.

I panicked. I knew that if there were a moment of delay, I would simply back out. I would keep the books, find a place to store them in our new apartment in New York. I had prepared myself emotionally to let go of these books on March 30, 2018. Not a day later.

"Oh, please, try to make it. I am afraid that if you do not come tomorrow, I will simply not have the courage to let them go."

At 9 a.m. the next day, Zeke Levine and Raphi Halff came to the office. By noon, my entire Yiddish collection was out of my office in their van. My office looked barren.

I felt the absence of those volumes, but I was thrilled to find out later that my set of I. J. Singer books were added to the vault of rare books at the Yiddish Center. I had selected them decades before, and now they had a new home where they would be loved and read. Like the people that I had selected for my society, they were the foundation for my success as a president.

CHAPTER 8

Both Ends of Remembrance

Remembrance has a Rear and Front—
—Emily Dickinson

Ceremony, commemoration, and celebration are important for a community. During my years as president at TCNJ, some of these events were annual, those marking the beginning of the year (Freshman Convocation and the Welcome Back Address), and those marking the end of the year (Senior Toast and Commencement).

The Fall Freshman Convocation was part of a formal orientation for the incoming freshman class. It marked the last day of Welcome Week for the new students and the first day of classes of their freshman year. Faculty, administrators, and trustees donned academic robes. The student body president, the faculty senate president, the president, and the provost greeted the students. The president of the Alumni Association welcomed students with a ceremonial exchanging of class banners, and an Alumni Association greeting.

In my charge, I always contextualized the event in the history of the institution, harkening back to TCNJ's origin as the New Jersey State Normal School, the first state public institution in New Jersey in

1855. I cited the institutional commitment to diversity and to being an "open, inclusive, and welcoming community where leadership is a shared responsibility and privilege." I reminded the students that this responsibility was a difficult negotiation of conflicting discourse and acknowledged that the enterprise was particularly challenging in these times of "extremism, intolerance, and partisanship." This message became more and more important over the years.

After the ceremony, the students walked through a gauntlet of applauding faculty, staff, administrators, and trustees to their first meetings with their respective deans. They were on their way to a four-year journey to a baccalaureate degree. Unlike many other institutions, at TCNJ, this *is* a four-year journey. The 2016 to 2017 annual report indicated that 75 percent of first-time full-time TCNJ students graduated in four years, one of the highest four-year graduation rates of public institutions in the nation. The national average graduation rate between 2008 to 2020 was 60 percent, and that is based on a six-year, not a four-year graduation time frame.

During the first week of the fall semester, after the welcoming of the new freshman class, I would greet the full campus community in a Welcome Back address, followed by a festive picnic on Green Lawn, the wooded area behind the administration building (Green Hall). That address included the requisite citation of the successes of the year before, but also sought to place the current moment of The College within an historical timeframe. For instance, on August 28, 2013, I marked the fifty-year anniversary of the Reverend Martin Luther King, Jr.'s speech on the steps of the Lincoln Memorial and its importance to our work at The College:

> [King's] soaring rhetoric and his hope for the future were inspiring, but that rhetoric and hope were ever-tempered by the harsh realities that surrounded him. Unfortunately, many of those circumstances surround us today. A remarkable aspect of King's leadership was that in the face of these realities, he did not succumb to pessimism

or political expediency; instead, he persevered. He persevered with integrity and commitment, a quality that should be both an inspiration and a challenge to us.

I used the anniversary as a platform for sharing with the audience where I thought The College had succeeded and where we had not, particularly in the characteristics of the freshman class. The students had great talent and had accomplished impressive achievements, but the class was not as diverse racially and ethnically as we had hoped it would be. While there had been significant growth in applicants from underrepresented groups, there had not been an increase in the number of Black or Hispanic matriculants.

In that year's updating of the strategic map for The College, diversity was a singular focus for the future, not just having students, faculty, and staff apply to come to TCNJ, but also in getting the students, faculty, and staff to choose TCNJ, to help them remain at TCNJ, and to help the students from all groups graduate on time. As a public institution in the state of New Jersey, we simply had to transform more of those diverse applicants to matriculants. It was a moral and civic responsibility.

Commencement was an equally important ceremonial point of the year. It was a time to celebrate student accomplishments, to thank families who supported those students and to honor the faculty who helped the students succeed. It was a time for the students to see their experience through a different lens, again quoting Emily Dickinson. This time I alluded to the greater acuteness of a "departing light" which clarifies experience through its special rays.

Just as in the Welcome Back address, I sought to contextualize the moment historically, citing major experiences that had marked the students' four years at TCNJ. For instance, in 2010, I noted events both national and local, extraordinary, and mundane:

> The national and international news headlines over the years of your time at The College reflect the seismic changes of our era. When most

of you arrived on the campus in 2006, the country was beginning the recovery process from the devastation of Hurricane Katrina. That year marked the deaths of Gerald Ford, James Brown, and Steve Irwin, the Crocodile Hunter. Other headlines included the election of the first female Speaker of the House, Nancy Pelosi, and the trial and execution of Saddam Hussein. In 2007, we saw the Dow Jones grow to over 14,000, the world of technology was enhanced with the release of the iPhone, the final *Harry Potter* book was released, and the country mourned the tragedy that occurred at Virginia Tech. 2008 was marked by an economic recession that has been compared to the Great Depression, and Bernie Madoff was arrested for one of the biggest Ponzi schemes in history. 2008 also brought us the election of the nation's first African American president, Barack Obama, and the World Champion Philadelphia Phillies. In 2009, we witnessed the miraculous landing of a commercial airliner on the Hudson River, the birth of octuplets, and the deaths of Walter Cronkite, Farrah Fawcett, Michael Jackson and Eunice Kennedy Shriver.

These events colored the experience for these students and provided both a beginning and an ending, a front, and a rear of their memories.

Over the years, the evening before commencement was the date on which the senior class would hold a dinner dance. The tradition of Senior Week (which was more like Senior Three Days) began in 1998. Seniors would return for a programmed couple of days, reliving their times in Travers-Wolfe. Over time, the programming included a special speaker, a picnic, and a trip to either an amusement park or the shore. The idea was a wonderful one, an opportunity for students to bond as they left their alma mater and set out on their adventures after graduation, entering the ranks of alumni.

But over the years, programming became less the attraction, and the opportunity for outrageous and, in some cases, destructive behavior became the goal for many students. Alcohol drove everything, and destruction of property and personal safety became an issue. For safety and ethical reasons, the program had to be significantly modified. Senior Week 2007 was canceled because the year before, one of the halls in Travers-Wolfe had been transformed into a Slip 'N Slide. It was brought back the next year, but with significant limitations on alcohol, which were only partially honored.

By 2014, the program became a legacy event that culminated the evening before commencement with a presidential toast and a senior gala. The Senior Toast was a time at which I could address the students in a way and tone that let them know that I was no longer thinking of them as students. My words were always tongue-in-cheek and meant to inspire them to be the best that they could be, but in a language that they had not yet heard from me. In 2013, for instance, I mused with the soon-to-be alumni about the special words and experiences for the Jersey experience (shore versus ocean; navigating a jug handle; the difference between North Jersey and South Jersey.) I ended with a series of wishes for their future:

1. Always stay in the right lane to exit the circle.
2. There are 565 different municipalities in the state of New Jersey and, God bless them, each and every one of them has its own rules and regulations, not to mention its own mayor, city council, or whatever.
3. Never get off the turnpike at 13A unless you have to fly out of Newark airport.
4. There really is a difference between North and South Jersey, but less than the difference between Jersey and most every other state in the nation.
5. Great pastrami comes from New Jersey, not New York.
6. Diversity is more than dark hair.
7. Politics *is* a blood sport.

8. Being cheeky and "in your face" is the best way to survive in this complex world.
9. We are *not* the *Jersey Shore*, but we love the Jersey shore.
10. Be proud to be someone who knows the power of love, the meaning of spirit, the agency of courage and thoughtful risk, and the joy in making a difference in the world.

While the modifications to Senior Week mitigated the behavioral problems, over the years, the community seemed to lose interest in continuing the tradition. Now, "Last Night on the Lake," held the night before commencement, sponsored by the senior class and the Alumni Association, has replaced the previous program. While I regret some of the changes that needed to be made in Senior Week, the changes were necessary.

There are also ceremonial events which are important for institutional memory that are singular, some to commemorate a loss (of an individual student or faculty member, the multiple anniversaries of 9/11). For instance, on August 18, 2007, we held an interfaith prayer service to mark the horrific loss at Virginia Tech University. I compared Virginia Tech's loss to what TCNJ had experienced the year before, after George Smith's death:

> Although we cannot comprehend the devastation that campus community must be feeling, we can sympathize with them as they begin the grieving process under the watchful, and in some cases, intrusive, eye of the public . . . Imagine how much more of an imperative it should be when that loss is of the magnitude in Blacksburg. As we learned during our tragedy last spring, privacy of personal grief is not always something that is respected and protected by the public.

I acknowledged my own anger not only at the magnitude of the loss at Virginia Tech, but also at the insensitivity of those who passed judgment on actions or lack of action on the campus. I reminded the audience that while the sheer number of deaths at Virginia Tech added to the loss, in the end, "loss is always individual. Loss is painfully about one person, suffered by each individual, and each individual mourner experiences that pain alone." There will likely be some solace for the mourner, but we as observers should "modestly help the Virginia Tech mourner find a way back to life. Our words and our prayers provide that safe and private space where the mourner can be restored by his own angel." I sought to express our solidarity with the Virginia Tech community while at the same time honoring our own loss, to remember and also to look forward.

Whenever a current student died, we established a tradition at TCNJ of outreach to the student's family, including my personal call to the family. The administration would offer to hold a service on the campus to memorialize the student should the family wish such a ceremony. Most often, those services were held in the Spiritual Center in the residential quadrant of the campus, and while the family often requested that religious observance be part of the event, families were most generous in allowing the time to be a moment for the deceased student's college friends to mourn in their own unique ways. I would usually make short remarks, but the focus was on those who knew the student best; the ones whose loss was greatest. My role was to provide the imprimatur of the institution in celebrating the life and remembering the individual. These sad events helped the individuals and the community heal.

Equally as important were the individual purely celebratory events, such as those associated with my inauguration, the sesquicentennial year of The College, and the 2018 celebration of my tenure as president.

Almost one year to the day of the vote of the Board of Trustees that confirmed my appointment, I was inaugurated as the fifteenth president of TCNJ. The ceremony and the gala that followed were the culmination of a week of panels, presentations, and discussions organized by faculty across the campus focusing on the theme of the five-day celebration, "Embracing the Future: The Changing Face of Leadership." Speakers included representatives from the US Department of State and the British Parliament, faculty from Columbia, Rutgers, and Princeton, Betty Williams, the 1976 Nobel Peace Prize winner, as well as presentations, art exhibits, and concerts by TCNJ faculty and students. These panels, exhibitions, and concerts celebrated the promise of the institution and characterized what could be offered by a high-quality public institution.

Mick Ferrari, former president of Drake University, then Chancellor of Texas Christian University, delivered the welcome from the academy at the inauguration, remarking "how fortunate The College of New Jersey is to have at its helm at this eventful time in its history, a person of extraordinary qualities who will lead The College to even greater beauty and prominence, not only within this community and state, but within the country and the world."

While I got a cranky letter from one alumnus regarding my choice (expressing concern that since I was Jewish, I would always choose a rabbi rather than a minister for public events), I was thrilled that Rabbi Randi Musnitsky, a female rabbi from Cherry Hill, could provide the invocation and benediction. It sent a message that I strongly identified both as a woman and as a Jew. The next week, I received a beautiful letter from the rabbi commending the ceremony and particularly noting my words at the ceremony: "You touched our hearts and motivated our spirits. May you enjoy this new era of excitement and growth under your leadership."

My own remarks at the inauguration were a combination of personal and professional touchstones, as a means of revealing myself to the community. I cited my sudden birth, some three weeks early, that required my mother to give birth at home; I referenced my mentors from my days at Drake, Oswego, Warrensburg, and Chapel Hill—many of whom were in the audience, the rest of whom were there in spirit. I missed the physical presence of my mother, my grandmother, my Aunt Flo, Hugh Holman, and so many others who had shaped my life, but the fact that my father was there was wonderful. There are some absolutely delightful photos of him dancing with me and the children at the inaugural gala, him smiling and swinging his cane. I ended my inauguration remarks challenging all in the audience to heed Stephen Spender's words to "think continually of those who were truly great."

Dear friends captured the warmth of the celebration. Lucy Blackburn, from Central Missouri State University, wrote an email to "Inaugurated Prexy Bobby," calling the event a "lifetime memory," and in a letter, she celebrated how much our relationship meant to both of us: "I do understand how much you love and appreciate me. That's how I feel about you."

In an email, Mick wrote, "I can't express adequately how impressed Jan [his wife] and I were with your inauguration, the beauty of the TCNJ campus, and the quality of people we met during our visit."

Wayne Pond, my office mate from Chapel Hill days, took a less serious tack: "It was *wonderful* to visit, see you crowned, and generally hang out at the inaugural festivities. (If there were glitches, you kept them well hidden.) Best of all, it was nice to hear all those good things that everybody said about you because you earned them. Wouldn't Hugh [our shared graduate mentor] be (isn't he) proud? . . . You need to cook up an excuse to visit UNC. When you do, we'll carry your scepter and robes and take you around, right?"

The TCNJ comments were welcoming and gratifying. The faculty and students seemed reassured by the tone of the festivities, the openness and inclusivity, the sense of humor and humaneness. Faculty celebrated what a new relationship with administration would mean. For instance, Anntarie Sims, professor of communication studies, wrote that my "genuine regard, warm concern, inclusion of all (faculty, staff, administration, students, and alumni) has rarely been done on our campus." The festivities captured what I hoped would characterize my tenure, focusing on the academic core of the enterprise and on the feeling of community. They celebrated the past while looking toward the future.

The academic year 2004 to 2005 marked the 150th anniversary

of the opening of the New Jersey State Normal School, TCNJ's first institutional name. The yearlong celebration began with a September 8, 2004 torch run through Trenton and Ewing; on Founder's Day (February 9, 2005), there was a scavenger hunt; students traveled to Rockefeller Center to stand behind the hosts on the *Today Show*; there was a huge birthday cake celebration in the student center; a time capsule was buried under the site for the new library. A symposium in honor of the sesquicentennial celebration of Walt Whitman's *Leaves of Grass* was held on September 22. On October 30, there was a Grand Finale Presidential Brunch for the entire community.

The goal was to consolidate community, create pride, commemorate the past, and look forward to the future. Every constituent group participated—trustees, alumni, local politicians, faculty, staff, and students. Just as the torch run marked the physical move from downtown Trenton, the additional events of the year marked the transition of the New Jersey State Normal School to the New Jersey State Normal School at Trenton, to the New Jersey State Teachers College and State Normal School at Trenton, to the New Jersey State Teachers College at Trenton, to Trenton State College, to The College of New Jersey.

During the twelve months between the announcement and the reality of my 2018 retirement, there were touching moments of celebration, commendations from the Faculty Senate, the Student Government, the New Jersey Legislature, and many personal letters. Faculty and staff often cited my position as mentor and inspiration, not just to women, but to young staff as they embarked on careers in higher education. Carol Evangelisto, a counselor at The College, wrote how much she admired me not just "as our beloved President, but as a woman, as a mother, as an educator, as a gifted public speaker . . . and as an all-around 'good citizen' . . . I will also never forget how in the very sad times in the College's history, you led us through with dignity, compassion and wisdom . . . Thank you too for your wonderful sense of humor that you also so generously shared."

Michael Beachem, a new residence hall director in my first years as president, wrote that he saw me as a "great role model and colleague." Nick Montesano (who paid his way through a TCNJ baccalaureate by working with Sodexo and was often present at the president's house as we hosted students, faculty, staff, and alumni) thanked me for what I had done for him: "You are truly an inspiring and remarkable person who has changed so many lives." A senior staff member from the Development Office, Jim Spencer, wrote, "I cherish the time I had to work with you. You are one of those individuals who has made a permanent, positive impact upon my life."

I also heard from distinguished alumni. Major General Maria Falca Dodson, who would become a trustee at TCNJ after my retirement, wrote, "It has been such an honor and pleasure to have known you, worked with you and watched your accomplishments unfold . . .Your dedication and commitment are what has truly transformed our college to the premier institution it now is." Tom Sullivan wrote that he and his wife were "just two of thousands of alum, students, and staff who love you for what you have accomplished in service to our world. It all comes from who you are. A refreshing light and humble source of leadership, energy and wisdom." Abby Wentworth Joseph, a student leader during my time as president, wrote, "Your contributions to The College over two decades have been extraordinary, and I have been so proud to know you and have you in my cheering section during that time. I believe that my association with my beloved alma mater will always be a strong one in large part because of your leadership during this period."

Some of the most gratifying comments were from board members. Miles Powell wrote, "I wanted to thank you for all of your support over my time as a trustee at TCNJ. It has been one of the great learning experiences of my career. While never cut from an 'academic cloth,' I have great respect for your ability to navigate that world with an eye toward its relationship with real world, i.e., economic concerns. You are an extraordinary woman and a great role model to so many. How blessed are you to have made such a profound impact on people and a place?"

Eleanor Horne had been on the Board of Trustees from 1985 to

1997 during my predecessor's tenure; she returned in 2009 and remained on the board during the remainder of my time as president. She wrote:

> It was a pleasure working with you and learning firsthand that effective leadership takes knowledge, incredible skill, energy, and compassion. It takes stamina, a strong sense of self and personal values, and a sense of humor . . . You changed an institution. You left it stronger than when you arrived. You did so, in part, by developing the people around you. You made it clear that TCNJ was more important than any of the personalities that worked or governed there. You set an example of marriage as partnership . . . In fact, the marriage is part of the framework for a demanding career.

But no one's appreciation would match that of the one person, other than Don, who really understood my job—Heather Fehn, Chief of Staff and Secretary to the Board of Trustees. On the heels of my retirement announcement, she wrote:

> While I realize you are still here for one more year, I also realize tomorrow will mark the beginning of a whirlwind of celebrations and goodbyes. I'd like to be among the first to what will undoubtedly be hundreds of people who will express their gratitude and appreciation . . . I do realize how fortunate I have been to have had a front row seat to your remarkable tenure as president. I've learned from every decision, every crisis, every celebration. I've learned how to lead with integrity and to expect the same of those around me. I've learned how to prioritize what is most important and to focus on accomplishing meaningful, impactful goals. Through all of this, I have also had the great benefit of learning from you what it means to be a wonderful wife, mother and daughter . . . We first met on August 18, 1998, in the lobby of the Newark Holiday Inn (at some ungodly hour!). While I knew then that we had found someone special, I had no idea what it would mean for TCNJ or

for me. Looking back over the last two decades, I have to admit how humbled I am to have had the honor of earning your trust and going through this journey with you.

There were two publications that preceded the formal celebration of my retirement and detailed the accomplishments of my nineteen years as president. The 2016 to 2017 College annual report provided a timeline and a series of major themes (academic transformation, both the curriculum and academic facilities, improving graduation rates, addressing sexual assault, navigating times of trouble, and celebrating diversity). The fall 2017 issue of the *TCNJ Magazine* included an article entitled "Our Notorious R.B.G." It was a comprehensive overview of my time as president, beginning with the memory I had shared with the reporter of my feelings about how I fit at TCNJ after that first airport interview. It captured much of what I wanted to be remembered for—the sense of deprecation that comes with being known by the students as "the Git," the fact that I loved to give credit to others when they were instrumental in a success. The article and the annual report articulated themes and successes that I hoped marked my tenure for others, but also provided a sense of celebration for the institution as a whole, an opportunity to both look backward and to look forward into the great promise of TCNJ into the future.

"Our Notorious R.B.G." included comments from colleagues and supporters. President of Princeton, Christopher Eisgruber, described me as "someone who has the heart and soul of a teacher and scholar. She's had one of the really successful college presidencies in the country." Former Governor Thomas Kean was quoted as saying, "There are a lot of college presidents who expanded the university, and some have helped with quality. Very seldom has somebody been able to do both. And she's done both in quite a remarkable way." Eleanor Horne commended my ability to handle difficult situations. "With Loser Hall, she acknowledged that this was important work for students to do, she trusted the process and carefully considered what was learned." In acknowledging the success of The College's first ever capital campaign, Jorge Caballero, the Chairman of the Board, told the reporter, "To me, it's a tremendous indication of the power of the leader and the power of the message that we have been able to deliver because of what she has done over the last eighteen years."

Students and staff put together an amazing series of scrapbooks which contain photographic memories of the 2017 to 2018 year. There are photos of students with "I heart the Git" posters and of staff members with "I heart RBG" T-shirts from the all-campus retirement celebration in front of the newly named R. Barbara Gitenstein Library. Words that were shared by faculty, staff, students and trustees became the post board at the gala, words that captured the qualities others thought I embodied: charismatic, insightful, empathetic, tireless, compassionate, dynamic, brilliant, honest, approachable, collaborative. They became the cover of a book commemorating the evening.

The weekend of March 16 to 18, 2018, was one of the most memorable of my life. The celebration itself was called "Portrait of a Presidency," echoing the title of the article ("Portrait of a President") that introduced me to the campus in The College magazine, some nineteen years earlier. Both sought to capture who I was. The original article provided background from my academic and personal past to help TCNJ learn who was going to be their president. It focused on my intellectual commitment to academic excellence, my love of art, music, and Emily Dickinson, and my amazing family.

The main celebration for my retirement was filled with videos and remarks by friends and mentors who had supported me over the years. Some of the video commendations made me glad that I had received the beautiful antique handkerchief from Amy Walton from the Development Office. Amy had been instrumental in planning the event, so she suspected that some of the comments would elicit tears and moments of surprise, many captured in poignant photos: me gasping when I saw my mentor, Don Mathieu, on the large screen, me leaning over to talk to my first grandchild, Ruby, who had crept onto her Abba's (Don's) lap.

Friends came from all over the country to celebrate with me and Don—both my upcoming retirement and my recent seventieth birthday. One of my dearest friends who came the farthest was my colleague from Drake, Pat Cavanaugh. He had served as Vice President of Finance at Drake and he and I had the best relationship of any provost and CFO that I have ever observed. We held each other accountable in ways that no one, not even the president, could do. We had high expectations of ourselves, of each other, and of Drake. He left the university before I did, for a second stint as CFO at University of the Pacific.

After he returned home, Pat wrote me a letter thanking me for being part of the celebratory weekend.

> The extent of your impact on the institution as presented in the presentations Saturday night is tremendous . . . but not surprising. I thought back twenty years when the Board at Drake decided to go with a former governor and retired insurance executive for all the wrong reasons. It was natural to speculate on what Drake would be today, if that decision was different . . . During the wonderful birthday party Friday evening and then again on Saturday, it was clear that you had the same impact on all the people who spoke . . . you made them all better people, and you made them proud of the things they accomplished with you by their side.

I was flattered by all this attention, but more importantly, I was humbled, because while I got so much credit, these successes were institutional successes, not individual successes, the result of collective work by a talented and generous team, not an individual.

While not a celebration for the community per se, the awarding of an honorary degree from Princeton University was a recognition not of me but of what TCNJ had come to represent in the years since my appointment. On June 5, 2018, I was awarded an honorary Doctor of Laws degree from Princeton University. The award was a surprise— for any number of reasons. First, after all, it was Princeton. Second, in 1996, Princeton had had a public legal battle with Trenton State College over who could use the name The College of New Jersey.

In the late fall of 2017 when I received a letter from President Eisgruber informing me that I had been "elected by the Trustees of Princeton University to receive an honorary degree at [its] Commencement in 2018 in recognition of [my] outstanding work in enhancing academic rigor and faculty-student engagement as the president of the College of New Jersey," I actually thought the letter was a hoax. Surely, I was not being considered as a candidate for an honorary degree from Princeton. But after a call to the president's office at Princeton, I wrote a letter accepting the election with gratitude, and then reached out, as instructed in the letter, to Robert Durkee, Secretary of the University, to confirm details of the day. There was something humorous about this contact, as it was Secretary Durkee who was the public voice of Princeton's objection to the college's name change in 1996.

The Princeton commencement was a wonderful experience for me. Don was joined by Pauline and Heather Fehn, my other daughter, as I had come to call her. The evening before the event, there was a dinner where I was able to meet the other awardees. They included Reverend Gregory Boyle, S.J., founder and executive director of Homeboy Industries in Los Angeles; Lonnie Bunch, III, founding director of the Smithsonian's National Museum of African American History and Culture; Robert Geddes, an architect and professor at Princeton; and Carla Diane Hayden, the Fourteenth Librarian of Congress. My citation read:

> This visionary leader is the first woman to serve as president of The College of New Jersey in the institution's 160-year history. Determined to provide her students with the highest caliber academic experience, she has led transformative efforts to improve TCNJ's four-year graduation rate, which now ranks among the highest in the nation for public colleges and universities. On a national level, she has been a steadfast advocate for academic rigor, high standards, and expanded educational opportunity.

Throughout her career, as a scholar of Jewish and American literature and as an insightful administrator, she has demonstrated the power of education to change lives and change the world.

What overwhelmed me that day were not the words of the citation, but the words that President Eisgruber added to his commencement remarks after the formal awarding of honorary degrees to the five recipients. In his comments to the 2018 Princeton graduating class, he charged them to commit to helping more students earn college degrees. He listed a series of actions and then concluded:

> A few moments ago, we awarded an honorary degree to President Barbara Gitenstein. Over her nearly two decades leading The College of New Jersey, she raised the College's four-year graduation rate from 58 percent to 75 percent, a number that puts TCNJ's on-time completion rate among the top ten in the nation for public colleges and universities. By raising TCNJ's graduation rate, President Gitenstein has improved the lives of thousands of students who might have left school with debt but no degree. Be an advocate for higher education leaders like Bobby Gitenstein, and for colleges like TCNJ that commit to improving completion rates.

The implication was clear: The honorary degree that I had received was not mine; it was TCNJ's. The success it recognized was the result of the work and commitment of an extraordinary faculty, a dedicated staff, particularly academic support staff, an indefatigable administrative team, and trustees who knew how to inspire, challenge, and ask the tough questions. We had accomplished a lot, and I was glad that we had been recognized for our work.

Like the other celebrations and commemorations that marked my time at TCNJ, the Princeton honorary degree had both a front and a rear. It spoke to what had been accomplished and what could be the promise for the future.

CHAPTER 9

Tell It Slant

Tell all the Truth but tell it slant—

—Emily Dickinson

The unrealistic part of me had hoped that the 2017 to 2018 academic year would be an easy one, a year filled only with joyous celebration and positive experience. No president of a complex organization should expect that. Much of the hard work of the last year of my presidency ended up being in follow-up to the difficult issues confronted by TCNJ the year before. As Emily Dickinson had established, the most powerful truth is always slant, because the brightness can be blinding.

First, there was the processing of the November 2016 election of Donald Trump. The shock and anger in the community was particularly apparent in the fall of 2016, but the undercurrent of distrust that permeated the country bled onto the campus. It undermined relationships between students and any person or entity of authority. In addition, there were specific episodes on the campus that exacerbated that sense of distrust.

In the fall of 2017, the final report of the Advisory Commission on Social Justice: Race and Educational Attainment was promulgated, though the most controversial recommendation (the changing of the name of Loser Hall) had already been announced at the end of the previous spring semester. One of the major recommendations was the implementation of actions to reconfirm The College's commitment to the city of Trenton through educational partnerships, led by a Steering Committee and Implementation Task Force with actionable initiatives. The goal of that recommendation was to address the advice that I had received from my colleagues, President Eisgruber and President DeGioia: to make sure that the work of the Commission created a platform for future progress in enhancing diversity rather than simply addressing the controversy of the name change of an academic building. These were all positive initiatives, but they were met with a good deal of suspicion by students.

There was one meeting with community leaders in the fall of 2017 which was supposed to be in follow up to these initiatives to reengage with Trenton and the local community. After a short presentation, a TCNJ student who had been born in Trenton stood to object to almost everything we were trying to accomplish. She was passionate about her advocacy for her community and disdainful of The College's attempts to reverse our reputation with Trenton. The community members were stunned at the anger and passion of the student. I was not. I do not believe that I convinced the student of the intent of our efforts, but I believe that I convinced the others in the room of the sincerity of our intent.

The Paul Loser controversy became intertwined with a largely unforced error to close the TCNJ Clinic. The clinic, administered out of the School of Education, which began as a convenient site for internships for graduate students in the counseling program, had grown into offering services not just for TCNJ students and staff, but also for needy community members. Dean Jeff Passe of the School of Education conducted a study in the early months of academic year 2016 to 2017 and, based on a financial analysis, recommended to the provost that the clinic be closed. Provost Taylor accepted the recommendation. Students and clients from on and off campus joined the director of the clinic and The Committee on Unity (TCU, a name echoing the name of the committee of city leaders who advocated for social justice in the 1950s) who were initially focused on the Loser Hall controversy to protest the closure. These groups saw the celebration of Loser and the removal of services for low-income students and neighbors as two examples of TCNJ's lack of concern for our surrounding community. In the April 26 issue of the *Signal,* the Director of the Clinic published an impassioned plea to keep the clinic open, arguing that the administration's substitution of a mental health partner did not adequately address the community need.

On May 4, 2017, as I had promised in my response to the demands from the students who took over the president's conference room, Student Affairs held an open forum for the community in the Brower Student Center. The large meeting room was filled: students, faculty advocates, and administrative leadership. Provost Taylor, Dean Passe, and I sat in the front row.

After an introduction by the Interim Vice President of Student Affairs, Angela Chong, Mark Forest, Director of Counseling and Psychological Services (CPS), gave an overview of the plans for future counseling at The College. Probably none of the students or faculty advocates listened to the presentation. They had already heard of the plans for the outside partner to support the work of The College's own Counseling Services, and they were not impressed. The presentation took about thirty minutes, and then Angela got up to help field and direct questions. It was clear that none of the student questioners felt as if they had received a valid reason for closing the clinic. None was moved by the argument that our first obligation was to our students, not the community.

"But even if, as you say, our focus is on our students," an English Department faculty member said, "my understanding is that the TCNJ Clinic provided lower cost services for our students than what is provided at CPS. How are you going to assure that our neediest students are not deprived of mental health services?"

A student in the back of the room stood up, crying, and said, "Yes, that's me. I can only afford to go to the TCNJ Clinic. Do you not care that I might kill myself?" There were gasps in the audience. Mark and Angela both interceded, sharing information about modified fees based on need.

After another hour of such questions, a student rose and said, "So, are you telling us that no matter what we say, you are going to close the TCNJ Clinic?" Provost Jackie Taylor stood up, turned around to the audience, and tried to make the argument of lack of financial viability for the clinic.

"So, you do not care what we say tonight. The decision has been made."

Jackie stood to answer, but before she could speak, I rose and interrupted.

"No," I said. "The final decision has not been made. We will absolutely take into account what you are saying tonight."

Six days later, I sent out a campus-wide memo indicating that I had accepted the provost's recommendation to delay the closure and "to implement a program review process for the TCNJ Clinic associated with the Counselor Education Program." In the fall, I announced the outcome of that review. I was accepting the provost's recommendation based on that review, "to create an incremental plan for incorporating the work of the current clinic into a center for health and wellness, a new entity with a larger scope." This October recommendation in essence reversed much that was embedded in the plan that was presented to the community at the May 4 town hall.

From the beginning, the school's decision-making process with regard to the clinic was problematic. The dean was inattentive to student concerns and was careless in engaging the administrative leadership of the clinic. The provost's response to the dean's recommendation was too deferential to the flawed process and did not reconsider her position by including additional input after the dean's recommendation. In the end, I concluded that I had to step in and reverse the decision, keeping the clinic open. While this decision was welcomed by the advocates for the clinic, overturning a decision by the dean (which was supported by the provost) was awkward and damaging. It undermined the provost, which I regretted; however, I believed that it was necessary to work toward reestablishing trust on the campus, particularly with underrepresented students and the larger Trenton community.

In my last Welcome Back remarks, I characterized the initiatives to restore a relationship with our community as a work in progress; the theme was so similar to that of my very first comments to the TCNJ community:

> If, however, we are going to succeed in any of these initiatives, we must learn to be better communicators—and that means listening as well as talking. In addition, we must forthrightly admit mistakes and missteps when they occur. I was disappointed at a number of junctures last year when it seemed as if we were eager to express our opinions and to assert our authority but not willing to engage in the hard process of productive action. It is simply not adequate to have our say—no matter who we are—administrators, faculty, staff, students, or alumni. In the end, we all belong to this community; we all have responsibilities as well as rights in the crafting of our future. That means that we must forcefully but civilly express our perspectives, but once that is done, we must allow others to do the same. And then we must do the hard work of social and community action and that work often entails compromise. No matter what we might see in the political realm, compromise is not a four-letter word, and it is not a weakness to review and reconsider when we come to recognize that our original plan of action is simply ill-considered.

While my last year was not trouble-free, all in all, I had a wonderful nineteen years as President of The College of New Jersey. I believe that the tenure would be deemed successful for a number of reasons. First, there are data points of success, the highlights of which were included in the 2016 to 2017 annual report referenced above (increase in academic reputation, increase in graduation rates, focused investment in physical plant, and a first ever successful capital campaign). Second was the length of my tenure. Finally, the context for my retirement was celebratory, not the result of a vote of no confidence from the faculty or a loss of trust from the trustees.

The American Council on Education publishes a survey of the American College President every five years or so. In the 2016 survey, the average length of service of a college president was six-and-a-half years; in the 2023 survey, the average length of service had dropped to 5.9; when I retired in 2018, I had served nineteen years. I chose when to step down; I was not forced out.

During that time, I learned a lot about myself, my strengths, and my weaknesses. I worked hard until the very end, confronting tough issues through the final year. I also learned some basics that are the foundation for a successful presidency.

1. Are You Right for the Job?

First and foremost, there must be "fit" between candidate and institution. The person who will flourish as president of Harvard will not flourish as president of a community college. The person who will flourish as president of TCNJ would not flourish as president of a largely commuter school like Montclair State University. This is a hard thing to determine, and sometimes it is not clear until after the job has been accepted.

It was pretty clear to me in that first off-site interview that I shared the values of The College, and that The College was looking for someone like me who was less interested in radical transformation based on beginning anew, and more interested in building on a strong foundation that would lead to long-term transformational and systemic change. Furthermore, as the higher education environment changed, The College, the board, and I were in sync on what we should do to meet the new challenges.

While it was never an important theme in our public relations, we knew that we had to grow in order to be sustainable, but that we could not grow without careful attention to providing support services to continue to improve success rates. I knew that it was important to heal the rift between TCNJ's past and its present in order to create a healthy future, to reconnect with alumni from the Trenton State College days and with Trenton itself. Like most significant challenges, this was not something that would be completed; it would always require attention. I knew that the special mission as a public academically competitive residential campus was a niche that TCNJ could hold, but only if we made important changes. Even as board members changed over the nineteen years I served, the board agreed and supported these goals.

2. Communication

Good communication makes for a successful leader. That means both speaking and listening. Sometimes the communication is formal, as in speeches and public emails and letters. Sometimes the communication is informal and individualized. I always responded to correspondence, and almost always personally. I sometimes referred to students "emailing while drunk," when I would receive crazy messages where the timestamp suggested the student had been spending more time partying than thinking about the issue. But I always responded, doing my best to take seriously the issue raised in the message.

I did the same with parents, some of whom were a little less gracious than their students. Sometimes these communications with parents were painful, as in the times when I called families after the death of a current student. Legislators, alumni, and donors could be difficult because they would sometimes make outrageous requests. I always responded forthrightly. Sometimes I had to tell the politician that while I would pass along the recommendation for a family member to work at TCNJ, I would not appoint them by fiat.

Communication during a crisis is the best example of when good communication can make a difference in an outcome and in the atmosphere of the campus. During the aftermath of 9/11 and of student deaths, I was always the voice that the campus heard. It was important for the community to know that I was involved and aware of the issues. I also was careful in a crisis to make sure that I did not overpromise or cover up the realities as I knew them. I made sure that the community was aware when I simply could not share details.

You cannot communicate well if you do not know your audience. Relationships with important stakeholder groups were essential. I had learned a great deal from watching Mick Ferrari about how to work with a board of trustees, but until you are the one in charge, the complexity of that relationship is not apparent. I sought never to surprise the board, particularly the board chair, but there were missteps. For instance, in 2004, I announced a major investment in need-based aid without fully vetting it with the trustees.

This was my first in the series of meetings with trustees for the year. The meeting with Bob Gladstone was early in the sequence as he was the chair of the board at the time. The meeting began with warmth and hospitality. When I walked into the back porch of his charming home in Belle Mead, I saw a beautiful display of sushi.

After some pleasantries, we sat down and then, "So, Bobby, tell me about this new Promise Award? What is the purpose and how are you going to fund it?" The tone had changed, and any appetite I had was gone. I could barely swallow.

Two months before, as an alumna of Chapel Hill, I had received a notice from my alma mater, announcing the Carolina Covenant, a financial aid package for all North Carolina students whose family income was lower than 200 percent of the federally defined poverty level. It was genius; it was inspiring; it was absolutely something we should mirror at TCNJ. I called the TCNJ CFO, Barbara Wineberg, into my office. "Barbara, I have a terrific idea." I pushed the slick announcement in front of her. She began to read and then asked for some time to get some sense of the cost for TCNJ.

Two days later, Barbara and I had a meeting. She had run the numbers; it was simply too expensive. The first year would not be so bad, but by the time we were supporting all students to graduation, the cost would be prohibitive, $9 million annually, Barbara calculated. Nine million dollars would represent almost 15 percent of our annual budget in 2003, and with likely tuition increases over the years, that total dollar obligation would grow, because we would have to increase the individual award to provide the same level of support for the student. I knew we could not do what I had hoped, but there had to be a modification that would create a program that helped the neediest attend TCNJ debt-free.

Barbara and I began meetings with representatives in Admissions and crafted the Educational Opportunity Fund (EOF) Promise Award. EOF is a New Jersey state-defined program that focuses its support on educationally and economically disadvantaged students (originally students from what used to be called the Abbott Districts). The Abbott Supreme Court ruling (in the 1980s) was named for the student on whose behalf the first case to change the formula for state funding for K–12 in New Jersey was brought. The ruling determined that needy districts came to be funded at a higher level than wealthier districts which could depend on more robust tax revenues to support school districts.

TCNJ's EOF Promise Award was crafted to provide financial support to EOF students at TCNJ for their first two years in addition to their state EOF funds. It was not as robust as the Carolina Covenant, but it was a start. Lisa Angeloni, Dean of Admissions, Barbara, and I were thrilled with our idea. The only problem was that I began discussing this huge new investment in public with no discussion with the board leadership or the Board Finance Committee. Talk about a speed bump! To their credit, the board leadership listened and agreed with the modified investment, chalked it up to a mistake by an ambitious and relatively new president.

Communication with faculty is equally as important as communication with the board. Though faculty cannot singlehandedly get rid of a president, a vote of no confidence by the faculty makes it hard to lead. During the 2006 threatened campus closure, I fully engaged the board but failed to communicate well with the faculty, causing unnecessary campus anger. Thankfully, the proposal was not necessary to implement, so the faculty anger diminished over time. Though the success of that was largely because of several vocal and thoughtful faculty who recognized that the proposal was only a last resort and should the state budget cut to TCNJ be minimized, it would be the first proposal to be dropped (as it was).

Staff communication is often unfortunately overlooked. One of the most helpful decisions I made during my tenure regarding good governance was to include staff more intentionally in the decision-making processes on campus—recommending to the board the addition of a staff representative to the Board of Trustees and creating the Staff Senate as an advisory body parallel to the Faculty Senate and the Student Government Association.

Finally, communication with students is the only way a president can be informed about the realities on the ground. Relationships with students were some of the most gratifying in my life as a president. Developing relationships with student leadership can be extremely important during times of crisis or student protest. These close relationships, however, have to have been developed before the crisis or protest. As I discuss below, some of this relationship development happens in the classroom, some in more informal circumstances.

3. Surround Yourself with Good and Talented People

The position of president is not a solo job. To be successful, the president should surround herself with good and talented people, those who share your values and admire what is best in you. They also must be willing and able to tell you when you are off track. These people begin with a supportive family. No one was more fortunate to have a supportive partner than I. Don Hart is an academic, intellectual, highly principled person who always advised me to do what sat at the core of my principles, never allowing me to be tempted by the expedient. It was extremely helpful that he understood the enterprise and that he knew my best self. It was also the case that Don made important friendships at Drake and at TCNJ, friendships that enriched our lives and helped inform my understanding of each institution.

My children, Pauline and Sam, were extraordinarily gracious in learning to grow up in an environment that put them in the spotlight when they likely did not relish that exposure. The fact of being their mother grounded me and helped me realize that the position was just that; it was not me; it was not my essence. I learned more from watching them navigate the complexity of such an upbringing than from any graduate course in leadership could have afforded me.

Throughout my career, I subscribed to the notion that a leader always hires talented people, individuals with special skills that balance the leader's skills, and people who are not afraid to disagree or to take thoughtful risks. Over time, I learned that it was important to consider diversity of perspectives as imperative to creating the team, and I do not mean diversity simply as a representational question—how many women, how many people of color, how many members of the LGBT community—but also diversity in perspectives and opinions. In fact, the differences of good colleagues who shared the commitment to the best interest of The College were often some of the most important reasons for my success. I had to be able to listen to a differing opinion and the members of the senior leadership team had to feel comfortable sharing those opinions.

I was fortunate to benefit from the support of:

1. Exceptional academics (two provosts, Steve Briggs and Jacqueline Taylor, who led the faculty discussions through difficult curricular and strategic planning processes)
2. Visionary CFOs (Barbara Wineberg and Lloyd Ricketts, who managed not just the budget during the most difficult times, but helped unwind a risky variable rate debt portfolio that had been implemented before my time)

3. Creative enrollment management leaders (Lisa Angeloni, who enhanced the student success rate while diversifying the profile demographically)
4. Talented fundraisers (John Donohue, who led TCNJ's first ever highly successful capital campaign and enhanced relationships with the local community)
5. Wise administrators of campus facilities and information resources (Curt Heuring, who, while following the outline of his predecessor Pete Mills, turned around a pattern of damaging budget overruns in facilities projects and put his own imprimatur on the campus, and Sharon Blanton, who brought the technological infrastructure of the campus into the twenty-first century)
6. Deft human resource professionals (Gregory Pogue, who helped me navigate some tricky personnel matters, guiding the institution when we needed to "add by subtraction")
7. Wise legal counsel that protected me and The College (Thomas Mahoney, who offered advice that spoke to my principles but kept me informed about implications of actions)

But nothing compared to the advice and support that I received from the individual closest to my daily work life, Heather Fehn, Assistant to the President and Secretary to the Board of Trustees. Heather understood the complexity of the enterprise. She understood the role and importance of a well-informed and fully engaged board of trustees.

When a president hires these good and talented people, she must make sure that she gives them space to do their job, to make mistakes, and to enhance the organization with their own particular talents. She must accept their advice, even when it does not at first comport with her expectations. There will be times when she will have to reject that advice, but she must make sure that they feel comfortable bringing her their best judgment and opinions. And always, she should make sure that they know that she wants to know when there is a problem, a possible catastrophe in the making.

An academic president should never forget the primary purpose of the place. She should not lose contact with faculty and the academic view. During my years as president, I came to depend on wise and well-respected faculty, some because of official positions, some because of unofficial positions (Michael Robertson, Amanda Norvell, Mort Winston, Rick Kamber, and Ralph Edelbach). There were moments in my tenure in which I owe success in a difficult situation largely to their input and advice. I never lost my identity as a faculty member. Unlike some of my colleagues, I did not regularly teach. I did often guest lecture in classes focusing on leadership courses in both business and women's studies.

Twice, I team-taught a course on topics closer to my disciplinary interests. The first was for the spring semester of 2000 with Ellen Friedman, Professor of English. It was wonderful to be back in the classroom engaged in conversations about Jewish-American Literature. It was inspiring to work with a master teacher who could challenge students to learn from literature in creative and imaginative ways. I came to realize, however, in that instance, that I could not focus on the classwork as the students should have expected because of my obligations as president. About two weeks into the class, on January 19, the Boland Hall fire at Seton Hall University in South Orange, New Jersey resulted in three student deaths and fifty-eight injured students. During the class hour, I found myself thinking about fire suppression safety in TCNJ's residence halls, not about Jerome Rothenberg's *Poland/1931*. One of the great outcomes of that experience, however, was a deep personal relationship with Ellen that has only grown over the years.

The second course I team-taught was a freshman seminar with Don. We tried to expose students to operatic versions of theater and novels (such as Verdi's *Othello* and Puccini's *Manon Lescaut*). We were only somewhat successful—partially because these were freshmen adjusting to the more demanding expectations of a college classroom, partially because none of the students in the class had chosen the course because of the topic or because of the instructor. It was just that the course fit into their academic schedules. Unlike with Ellen, I felt less guilt turning the class over to Don when the pressure of the president's job made it necessary to not grade papers or be absent from a class.

Throughout my tenure as president, I missed that special relationship that can only be developed between a classroom instructor and her students, but throughout my career at TCNJ, I found other ways to engage with students and learn from them, essential for presidential success. I met regularly with the student leaders (individually and in groups) who provided invaluable input. I often hosted events at 110 Murphy and in that more relaxed social environment, students were comfortable sharing their concerns and opinions, more so than at more formal events on campus.

There were also individual meetings with students that enriched my life and my leadership at TCNJ. I first met Rick Addante when he was a candidate for a Rhodes Scholarship. He asked for a meeting with me to get advice while preparing for the interview. I remember him taking notes assiduously as we talked—the importance of listening as well as talking, the balance of confidence and humility, the advice to drink white versus red wine (in case of spills). This was a young man who experienced both tremendous personal challenges and a wonderful mentorship (by TCNJ's renowned wrestling coach, Dave Icenhower). While he was not named a Rhodes Scholar, he eventually graduated from TCNJ and earned a PhD in Neuroscience from University of California, Davis. I am particularly indebted to Al Ribiero, who was student body president in September 2001. Al was the first person to say to me on that very sad morning, "The first thing we need to make sure of is that our Muslim students are not scapegoated."

The relationship of the president to the trustees must be nourished. Without board support, a president will not succeed, whether the board is self-perpetuating, politically appointed, or elected. This is particularly tricky, since this is the group over which the president has the least control. Trustees are the fiduciaries of the institution, and as implied in their title, they hold the institution "in trust." Considering the appointment process and the highly political nature of the state of New Jersey, TCNJ was fortunate in the membership of the board.

During my tenure, the board served as an excellent partner in leading The College, providing thoughtful and sharp input, asking appropriate and challenging questions, providing support in difficult times, and assuring that The College preserved its special mission. As I have already said, most of the board chairs during my tenure were exceptional partnering with me to lead through complex financial and real estate transactions, student and national crises, faculty complaints, and student protests. It is important for a president to create the culture on campus where strong trustees are encouraged to engage in important issues, raise tough questions, and feel comfortable raising concerns, but also realize that these actions are at the strategic and generative level, not at the management level.

4. Take Principled Stances and Make Tough Decisions

While it is not always easy, it is important for presidents to make important principled statements. When a leader speaks out on controversial topics, it must be with the recognition that the statements will not be met with universal commendation. When I pushed back on the community anger about Reverend White visiting campus, I knew that for me and for an institution like TCNJ which prized free speech, I had to object to the gut reaction that fueled some to argue against his being allowed on campus in the first place. As offensive as his opinions were, censuring his speech was not the answer.

In 2013, when Roland Martin was invited to campus, a group of faculty members raised objections to his presence to the provost because of his problematic comments that led to his being suspended by CNN. Without my knowledge, Martin was disinvited, but we were obligated to pay his fee. Once I found out about Martin's invitation having been rescinded, I reached out to his agent and reinvited him for the next year with the assurance of a second fee. In the same conversation, I let the agent know of the concerns on campus. Martin politely declined. It was an embarrassing situation, but it was the right thing to do.

About a year into my presidency, the US Department of Education informed The College that it would conduct an investigation into our reporting of sexual assault cases. The specific concern was what appeared to be an underreporting of cases in the 1996 to 1997 academic year. As it turned out, the problem was one of misidentification of types of assault, essentially a categorization error, not intentional underreporting.

After correcting the processes and providing a thorough report back to the Department, I determined that this would be a good platform for highlighting the scourge of sexual assault on college campuses and providing focus to develop programs to support victims. In 2003, we applied for and received a grant from the Department of Justice, and with the insights and support of a campus-wide Sexual Assault Task Force, The College developed a robust series of programs, including the establishment of the Office of Anti-Violence Initiatives and a revamping of our Title IX Office.

Largely because of this commitment, along with only five other college presidents, I was invited in April 2014 to be present at Vice President Biden's presentation of the findings from the White House Task Force to Protect Students from Sexual Assault. My decision to confront rather than bury the story of the Department of Education case was welcomed by students and most faculty. It was celebrated by colleagues and politicians who were interested in the topic. This commitment, however, did not come without controversy.

I had just entered the board room for the October 2004 Executive Committee meeting when I saw one trustee turn to another and ask why we were emphasizing this controversial topic. In my report to the Committee that day, I detailed our plans to enhance support programs for victims and likely victims of sexual assault. I emphasized the sad truth that sexual assault was one of the least reported crimes anywhere and particularly so on a college campus. My comments prompted the board member whom I overheard ask about the Task Force before the meeting to ask why we would want more students to report assaults. Wouldn't that bring us negative press?

I assured him that we were not encouraging students to be victimized but encouraging them to report that victimization. The point is, we should do our best to help normalize the reporting structure. The fact of the matter is that if we were successful, our numbers in the Clery Report would go up. It would not mean that there were more assaults, but that more victims felt comfortable coming forward, getting help, and allowing us to discipline perpetrators. I do not think that I ever convinced that trustee of the righteousness of my direction, but I know that every single female on the board agreed with me. The invitation to Vice President Biden's Task Force meeting proved that at least national attention was positive.

Some of my toughest decisions concerned personnel matters. Over the years, I had to facilitate the resignation or retirement of a few administrators. It was always important to gather as much input as possible without breaching confidentiality. I sometimes found it necessary to hire outside expertise, but most of the time, I did the work by myself, with the support of the human resources office. The goal was to come to the best decision for the unit and The College, but to do so in a way that preserved the dignity of the individual. These were never cases of illegal or immoral actions, but rather cases of not fulfilling duties at the level necessary for a high-quality organization.

Sometimes the individuals were given temporary positions in other offices across the campus. Sometimes they were given leaves to prepare for their next opportunity. Only one of the six or so such decisions ever gave me pause. In that case, perhaps more extensive coaching to grow in the job would have been the better decision, but the others were unquestionably the right decision for TCNJ and the divisions which they led.

5. Be Generous

It is often said that a good trustee gives in time, talent, and treasure. The same should hold true for a president. I would also add that a president should be generous with praise. Being a president is a twenty-four-seven job. Days extend into the early hours of the next day, sometimes with work brought home, and sometimes with social obligations at the presidential home. There were times when Don and I would host four events at 110 Murphy Drive in one week. It is important that at those events, guests know that you are pleased to be spending your time with them.

But more than the pressure of hours of socializing and working, the greater pressure was awaiting that call about the health and safety of some undergraduate student who had been in a car accident, or some group of students who were delayed by conflict in a war-torn Syria.

When I entered administration, I'd had extensive education in explication of a difficult Henry James novella, but little training in managing a $200 million dollar operation, with over 1,000 employees and 7,500 students, or navigating the complexities of New Jersey state politics. However, the intellectual skills that I developed as an academic, the fortune of observing a natural businessman, my father, and the blessing of numerous mentors from every place in my life honed my talent as an administrator. This kind of training also reinforced a sense of humility that allowed me to offer praise to those around me, to ask for help and advice, and to admit in public when I had made a mistake.

While not all my colleagues would agree, I also believe that a president should be generous with financial gifts to the institution you serve. More than likely, you have been given a healthy compensation package. Some of that should be reinvested in the institution, not just as a gesture of generosity, but also as a financial statement of support for the mission. Don and I established the Gitenstein-Hart Sabbatical Prize endowment to allow early career faculty to choose a full year rather than a semester sabbatical.

Expressions of appreciation from faculty who received this award were particularly gratifying because they understood that the gift was an acknowledgement not only of their scholarly promise, but also of how that scholarship would enrich their teaching. They knew that Don and I, as former faculty members, understood that having the opportunity to spend extended periods on the research of choice was at the center of the life of the academy. Deborah Hutton, Professor of Art, the fourth (2017 to 2018) Gitenstein-Hart recipient, wrote, "Sometimes, working as I do in the rather obscure field of Indian and Islamic Art, I can feel a bit isolated at TCNJ, but this award makes me feel part of a larger scholarly community in a way that is deeply gratifying."

It is important for the president to recognize that she did not accomplish anything without support from others. I relished giving public credit to faculty and students for their achievements. Such successes were proof of the success of TCNJ. Even more significant, while I might have been the voice for major initiatives and even the one who imagined the initiative, I never accomplished an initiative alone. The important point here, however, is not that I am expressing my appreciation for their work here, but that when they read these sentences, they will remember innumerable times when I expressed these same sentiments to them and to the public.

Part of generosity is actively engaging in the life of the community, including leading important moments of celebration and commemoration. Celebrations mark important moments in an institution's history. As I have written earlier—some are regularly scheduled annual events (welcome back and commencement); some are idiosyncratic (the inauguration and the celebration of my retirement). Some are very public (the inauguration, commencement); some are for a smaller audience (the annual holiday party at the president's home; the numerous dinner parties for student groups and alumni; the annual dinner to mark years of service and retirements). In every case, the celebration is about the institution. It is an opportunity for the leader to consolidate a shared vision of the community and to provide opportunities to celebrate individual achievements.

6. Separate Yourself from the Job and Keep a Sense of Humor

Being a president is a heady experience. I have observed some colleagues who got swept up in the pageantry and perks of the job. They began to believe that they *were* the president. Perhaps it was because I had children, but I always knew that I was in the role as president. I was not, in my essence, the president. That made it easier for me to understand when I was expecting too much of a colleague or falling for the pageantry of the job. I learned the importance of modifying requests when something would even have the appearance of impropriety, not just paying for services that could have been covered by The College, but also making a distinction between what I wanted and what I needed as president.

In addition, it is important to be aware of what you say or observe.

I learned a great lesson from Steve Weber when he was the new president at SUNY-Oswego. His office was on the seventh floor of the administration building. It was about 5 p.m., and everyone but the cleaning crew had left the building. A young man walked in. He was the janitor. Steve looked out the window of his office and observed the plantings on the ground below his office:

"It's a great view. Just noticed that some of those plantings look a little tired. I'll get out of your hair and let you clean."

Steve gathered his briefcase and left his office.

Two days later, Steve was looking out the same window. And there below, all new plantings.

The reason I even know this story is that Steve understood the difference between self and position, because he is the one who told me the story as advice to a new president to be careful what she says.

The fact that the students came to know me as "the Git" and The College magazine titled an article "Our Notorious R.B.G." gives some sense of how the community engaged with me on a personal level. It was not that they did not respect me; it was that they saw me as someone who took the job of president, but not myself, seriously. I could take a joke.

In my last year, the public relations office proposed a humorous goodbye gift to the community. They produced a video of me pursuing my own bucket list of things that I wanted to do, things that were well known to be on the bucket list of TCNJ students. They included:

1. Selfie with the Git (for my selfie, it was a large cardboard version of myself)
2. Reading by the lake (there are two iconic lakes on the campus surrounded by lovely wooden benches)
3. A high five with Roscoe (Roscoe is the name of the Lion mascot for The College)
4. Riding the Lion at West Library (there is a life size stone statue outside the older library building)
5. A high five with Larry in Eick (Larry was a beloved Sodexo staff member in Eickhoff dining hall)
6. Sledding on an Eick tray (the hills in front of Travers-Wolfe were great sledding places during snowstorms)
7. Running the loop (one of the favorite routes for student runners was the driving loop around the perimeter of the campus)
8. Jumping in the fountain in the Science Complex (such dunking was not allowed)
9. Waving from the clock tower atop Green Hall (Green Hall is the major administrative building)

Filming this video was some of the best fun I had as president, though the experiences had their challenges. When I jumped in the fountain, I was reminded that it was a pretty cold day in March. When the student photographer, Aaron Watson, called from the grove of trees way down on Green Lawn for me to give a wave, I looked down from the small ledge of the clock tower three stories above ground and gasped. I clasped my calves against the ladder propped against the fence surrounding the decorative balcony above the second floor. It was a long way down. I smiled and waved, and when he remarked about how brave I was, I responded, "Not brave, terrified!"

7. Know When to Leave

No one can predict what is in the cards for tomorrow, and surely the leader of a college cannot know what the next month brings, but if you can, try your best to leave on a high. Do not try to meet an artificial timeline—keeping the job until you are a certain age or completing a decade of service (a nice round twenty years would have been nice). Do not try to outlast your predecessor. Be aware that even if you leave on a high, those last months will be filled with both the regular problems invested in such a job and with the problems of transition. The more successful you were as a president, the more complex those problems of transition: You know that it's time to leave, but you love the place and find it hard to let go.

After retirement, I decided to move out of town, in fact, out of New Jersey, to assure that my successor would not feel any undue pressure from my presence, as I had felt for my entire tenure from my immediate predecessor. I still believe that was the best decision for both me and my successor, but even so, the separation was difficult.

Do not give into the temptation to reach out and meddle after retirement. You can always serve as a sounding board, but you should never get sucked into the temptation to substitute your opinion for that of the successor president. And let your successor initiate such outreach. You are no longer the president; you are not the institution. You were a temporary servant leader for the place you held in trust during the time of your tenure, and you must let go.

8. The Changing Landscape

As I am writing this volume in 2024, I acknowledge the landscape in higher education has changed from 2018. Confidence in the enterprise is at an all-time low. In July 2023, the Gallup Poll reported that the share of the American public with "a great deal" or "quite a lot" of confidence in the academy was only 36 percent. That's down from 2018 (48 percent), which was down from 2015 (57 percent). *Inside Higher Education* published an opinion piece, in which I wrote:

> The pandemic changed the way . . . institutions deliver education, the relationship between boards and presidents, and the connections between faculty and students. Meanwhile, partisan politics have become increasingly mean-spirited, and much of what is said on the right or left is unmoored from what we used to accept as shared facts. But we as leaders need to own that we are partly responsible for such changes. We have been entirely too passive and too silent for too long.

In the article, I emphasized that when I spoke out as president, I did so only when the topic or issue sat at the center of the mission of the institution. I made clear that it was important to consult and inform the board of any such statements. It was wise to consult and take input from other constituent groups in crafting such statements. It was inappropriate to take narrowly partisan stances. It was necessary to give space to others on the campus to disagree without discipline.

I reminded the readers that this was not the first time higher education leaders were being accused of lack of courage, but that the stakes were much higher than when journalists in the 1990s were calling for the new Ted Hesburghs and Clark Kerrs. I acknowledged that when a president takes strong stances, that leader should be prepared to expect disagreement on the campus and even more significantly on the board. Since leadership on moral issues was part of the job of being president, there are times when a president must simply accept the consequence of campus and board disapproval. Perhaps receiving a "pink slip. . . may very well be a badge of honor."

I want to underline that my article was written in the summer of 2023, before October 7, 2023, when the attacks on higher education leadership became a perfect storm from the right and from the left. We were already in the midst of the undermining of free speech and the integrity of the academy in states like Florida and Texas, but now the fight between the progressive left and the moderate left that came to be invested in individual interpretations of who was wrong (or who was the most wrong) in the Israel-Hamas war turned campuses into landscapes of antisemitic and Islamophobic chants.

Jewish students were said to be fearful of wearing stars of David and were attacked with flag poles; Muslim students were doxed and denied interviews at specific law firms; student groups were banned from campuses. And then, on December 6, three presidents of prestigious private institutions, two from the Ivy League, provided testimony to a completely unsympathetic and aggressively critical group of congressmen. The fuse was lit. The three presidents were undoubtedly pilloried unfairly, but their testimony was a disaster, and frankly, an embarrassment. They seemed to have been prepped by the same law firm, and they seemed completely unprepared for the kind of questioning and the harsh light. One of my colleagues, Michael Bernstein, now President of TCNJ, put it best: "Perhaps their staff had led them to believe that they were being invited to a garden party. But, in fact, they had been invited to a bar room brawl."

On April 17, the president of Columbia testified at a follow-up congressional hearing, and while her responses were significantly better than her colleagues, her comments were an overcorrection in many ways. She did forthrightly address the fact of antisemitic statements that were part of the narrative of the campus protests, but I feel she too easily gave over to the attack on free speech and the autonomy of faculty voice in the American academy.

It should not go without notice that all three of the presidents at the first hearing (the most contentious) were women. I doubt that a man would have been treated with the same disdain and condescension. In addition, these presidents were all from the most selective private institutions. I doubt that their day-to-day interactions with politicians is as well-honed as that of any president from a public—particularly, any flagship—institution. The hearing on May 23 largely proved my point here. All the presidents on the hot seat were men; two were from public institutions. While the congressmen were no more sympathetic to the nuance, the tone of the hearing was entirely different. There was actually some grudging deference to President Holloway (Rutgers), President Schill (Northwestern), and President Bloch (University of California at Los Angeles). Most significantly, the presidents to a person felt more comfortable standing firm on their stances, defending their decisions to negotiate with the student protesters, to delay bringing in outside police forces. They acted like the higher education leaders that they were. The systemic sexism in the treatment of these higher education leaders is further underlined by the impact on the careers of the seven presidents who testified before Congress. Within eight months of the first hearing, of the seven presidents who testified, three have resigned. All are women, two are women of color. Within months of the May hearing, another president had resigned. He was the only president on that panel who was a person of color.

The entire conversation about what is currently happening at institutions is much too focused on the Ivy League, where fewer than .5 percent of the undergraduate students in the United States attend. Even so, what I suggest in this book about being forthright, speaking up when it makes sense, still pertains. I submit that such speaking out is happening on college campuses, probably more so at the publics than ever hits the press. The presidents who testified on May 23 were more in keeping with that recognition. I worry that the fear of the attacks that are currently overwhelming college leaders will lead them to be even more timid at just the time when we need them to be more courageous.

As I say above, a president should speak out on controversial topics but should at the same time assert the centrality of free speech. Reverend White and the Bible Believers did not represent the values of TCNJ, but silencing them by refusing their right to speak on campus would be a direct attack on the bedrock of American higher education, academic freedom and free speech. Furthermore, the calling in of outside safety agencies, such as municipal police, must remain the last resort by a president. There are so many steps before such action should be taken. The president and senior administration simply must engage in that difficult and sometimes unpleasant conversation with those who disapprove of your stance, but the people you should be speaking to are your students. It is your responsibility to do everything in your power to make even these conflict-ridden discussions a learning experience. This point is entirely missed by the congressmen who took the presidents of Rutgers and Northwestern to task for doing just that—working with and listening to their students. And again, once your position is represented by police decked out in riot gear, there is no time for conversation.

I do not have to be comfortable with the slogan "from the river to the sea," chanted by pro-Palestinian student protestors, but the phrase by itself does not imply death to all Jews. On the other hand, if there is clear evidence that some group explicitly espouses genocide against Jews, then it is not a leap of faith to interpret that as antisemitism and by such a definition a type of hate speech. This holding of two views is not only possible for a president of an institution of higher education, but also necessary at this time. And it is a view that should be said out loud.

AFTERWORD

The transition from serving as president to any new role is not an easy one. I suspect that it would be different for someone who transitioned from one presidency to another, but I simply stepped down into retirement. In 2018, I thought that I would embrace my newfound freedom from responsibility. How could I be seventy years old and know so little of myself?

At the beginning, I did love being in control of my calendar, of lazy wake-ups and early-to-beds, but I became bored. I became more acclimated to my new status when in the fall of 2018, I threw myself into the writing of my first memoir, *Experience is the Angled Road: Memoir of an Academic* (Koehler Books: 2022). I also enjoyed opportunities to work as a consultant for the Association of Governing Boards (AGB), offering input and advice to colleagues and their boards of trustees, but once the book was placed, I began to feel restless.

In Fall of 2021, I accepted the position of Senior Vice President for Consulting at AGB, where I was able to provide leadership in reestablishing a professional staff, structure, and foundational operating procedures for the consulting arm of the association, but after eighteen months, I concluded that someone else should take the department into the future.

In my second retirement from full-time work, I was more content with the change in the pressure of a day and turned my attention to a more focused consulting practice (on best board governance practice and coaching and mentoring of senior executives) and writing this book. This time around, I knew more of what to expect, and I was more prepared for the long downtimes and the greater quiet. I think retirement will stick this time.

I add this, looking backward to counsel my colleagues, that leaving a high intensity job like president of a college is harder than you think. At first, you believe that you will embrace the quiet wholeheartedly, and many of my colleagues have done just that. But for some of us, those who are perhaps adrenaline junkies, the quiet and unpacked calendar is not entirely welcome.

I had to figure out how to get over that addiction and to release my need to know everything about a complex organization, to be in charge of that organization. I am not sure that I can declare that I have overcome those needs, but I believe that I am in the process of overcoming them. I will always love TCNJ and will always feel that pull to engage in its challenges and promise, but I think I am learning to let go.

ACKNOWLEDGMENTS

There are many people to whom I am indebted for this book. The book is a testament to that debt. There is no way I could have succeeded without members of the TCNJ community, some of whom are cited in Chapter 9: Tell It Slant, section 3. Surround yourself with good and talented people. I would be remiss if I did not thank the support and advice shown to me throughout my nineteen years at TCNJ by the trustees and the members of the Foundation and Alumni Boards. The students at The College are a special breed and give me confidence in the future of the world; the faculty is world-class, and the staff is talented and professional, deeply dedicated to the mission of TCNJ and the power of higher education.

There are, however, certain individuals who must be called out because of the specific input they provided in the writing of this volume. These include my colleague from Duke days, Peggy Payne, who provided invaluable advice on the shape of the book; Tom Mahoney, Tim Grant, and Michael Robertson, who provided important guidance on details of the narrative. Heather Fehn was instrumental in answering questions and providing information large and small that greatly enhanced the book. My agent, Nancy Rosenfeld, as in the past, served as a great reader of the text and guide through the publishing world, and all the people at Koehler Books did masterful jobs in getting the book to print, including Nina Correa White, Lauren Sheldon, and Becky Hilliker. My children (Pauline and Sam) were generous in their support of my writing the sections of the book that focused on periods in their lives that were very difficult. And finally, Don, to whom this book is dedicated, there are not words to thank him, for everything.

www.ingramcontent.com/pod-product-compliance
Lightning Source LLC
LaVergne TN
LVHW041945070526
838199LV00051BA/2916